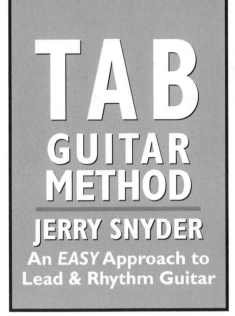

TAB GUITAR METHOD

JERRY SNYDER

An *EASY* Approach to Lead & Rhythm Guitar

C000145655

The **TAB GUITAR METHOD** is an easy approach to *lead* and *rhythm* guitar. It provides you with a thorough introduction to tablature, chords, standard music notation and music fundamentals. Of the 34 songs in the book, 30 are original and were written to present a variety of styles, which includes pop, rock, Latin, country, jazz and blues.

CONTENTS

ISBN 0-7390-2265-2
ISBN 978-0-7390-2265-8

Cover photo: Ken Hanson
Cover design: Martha Widman

TYPES OF GUITARS

You can learn to play the guitar using any one of several types of guitar: *steel-string acoustic, nylon-string classical, solid-body electric, or a semi-hollow body electric*. The important thing is that the guitar be properly adjusted for ease of playing. The most critical adjustment is the so-called "action." Action refers to the height of the strings above the fingerboard. If the action is too high, the guitar will be difficult to play. The gauge of the strings on the guitar also contributes to the ease of playing. Gauge is the diameter of a string, measured in thousandths of an inch. For example, the 1st string can vary in string gauge from .008 (light) to .014 (heavy). A guitar with high action and heavy strings will discourage even the most enthusiastic beginner. Make certain that in the beginning, your acoustic or electric steel-string guitar has light gauge strings on it. If you are playing a nylon-string classical, I would recommend light, normal or medium tension strings.

As a beginner, the selection of a guitar is a matter of personal preference. The primary difference between the various guitars is *tone quality*. Competitive prices have brought both acoustic and electric guitars into a reasonable price range for the beginner.

Acoustic Guitars (unamplified)

STEEL-STRING GUITAR. Manufacturers also describe this guitar as a *flat-top guitar* or a *folk guitar*. The body of the guitar is hollow with a flat top, a round soundhole, a pin-type bridge, and a pick guard. The neck is fairly narrow and normally joins the body at the 14th fret. The tone quality is bright, brassy and forceful, and lends itself perfectly to folk, country, ragtime, blues and pop styles. Beginners should put light gauge strings on their steel-string guitar for ease in playing. Bronze strings with ball ends are recommended. The guitar can be played with a pick, with the fingers, or with the thumb and finger picks (fig. 1).

fig. 1. Steel-string guitar.

NYLON-STRING CLASSICAL GUITAR. Referred to as the *nylon-string guitar, classical guitar* or *folk guitar*, this guitar is strung with nylon strings. This contributes to its fast action and ease of playing. The body is hollow with a flat top, it has a round soundhole and a stationary loop-type bridge. The neck is wider than that of a steel-string guitar. One of the distinguishing characteristics of this guitar is its open peghead. The tone quality might be described as dark, mellow and delicate. This guitar has a rich repertoire of classical music but is also suited for pop, folk, latin and jazz. The nylon-string guitar is played fingerstyle; that is, the strings are plucked with the fingers of the right hand. Never put steel strings on a nylon-string guitar (fig. 2).

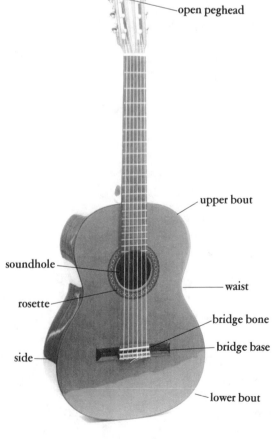

fig. 2 Nylon-string guitar.

ACOUSTIC/ELECTRIC GUITARS. The acoustic steel and nylon string guitar have also gone electric. *Acoustic/electric guitar* is the best description for what is now possible with the use of various magnetic, contact and transducer type pick-ups which amplify the sound. Some of these pick-ups can be attached to the guitar and some are actually built into the guitar.

Electric Guitars

SOLID-BODY ELECTRIC GUITAR. Without amplification, this guitar is too soft to be heard even for practicing. It relies almost entirely upon the pick-ups and amplifier. The body is solid and comes in a variety of shapes and designs. It has a thin neck and a "cut-away" design to enable the player to play in high positions. In regards to tone quality, there is an emphasis on the trebles (highs); however, a wide variety of tone qualities are possible. There is sustaining power due to the solid body which absorbs less energy from the strings than does an acoustic or semi-acoustic guitar. This is a favorite guitar with blues and rock guitarists.

fig. 3   Solid-body electric guitar.

fig. 4   Semi-hollow body electric guitar.

SEMI-HOLLOW BODY ELECTRIC GUITAR. The body of this guitar is thin and semi-hollow. It has an arched top and back, F-holes and a pick guard. The neck is thin and is attached to the body at the 18th fret. This guitar has a wide range of tone qualities ranging from a fairly dark and mellow sound to the more treble sound of the solid-body electric. Without an amplifier, this guitar can barely be heard. The semi-hollow body lends itself well to country, rock, pop and blues styles. It has good sustain and can be played at high volumes without feedback problems.

Amplification

A small practice amplifier will be necessary if you begin on an electric guitar. For home practice, a 10-watt amplifier with a 10-inch speaker will be more than adequate. Manufacturers have even smaller practice amps available that may suit your needs. Recently, several companies have developed earphones that can be plugged directly into your guitar. The earphones run on a nine-volt battery and are the cheapest solution to amplifying your guitar.

4

HOLDING THE GUITAR

Playing positions vary somewhat with the type of guitar, style of music performed and the right-hand technique being used. There are, however, some basic similarities that are important to observe if you are to develop a good left- and right-hand technique. Study both of the following descriptions.

Sitting Position

Place the waist of the guitar on the right thigh. Tilt the guitar slightly toward you. Keep the neck of the guitar at a 15 degree angle to the floor. Rest the forearm on the edge of the guitar at a point just above the bridge base. Bring the left hand up to the neck of the guitar. The wrist should be kept straight except when playing chords. When you play chords, arch the wrist slightly toward the floor. Never rest the left forearm on your knee or leg (fig. 1).

fig. 1 Sitting position.

Standing Position

A strap is used to hold the guitar when you are standing. Some guitarists even prefer to use a strap when they are sitting. Acoustic guitar straps are generally attached to a pin on the end of the guitar and the head of the guitar just above the nut (fig. 2). Electric guitars usually have a strap button mounted on the body of the guitar in addition to the end pin (fig. 3).

fig. 2 Standing position.

fig. 3 Standing position.

RIGHT-HAND PLAYING TECHNIQUE

A **PICK**, also called a *flat-pick* or *plectrum*, is used to strum or pick the strings of the guitar. Picks come in various sizes, shapes and thicknesses, and are made out of many different kinds of material including plastic, nylon, tortoise shell, rubber, felt and stone. Manufacturers describe the *gauge* or thickness of their picks as light, medium and heavy. I recommend that beginners use a pear-shape or drop-shape pick with a medium size and thickness (fig. 4 and 5).

fig. 4 Pear shape

fig. 5 Drop shape

Hold the pick between the thumb and index finger. The pick should rest on the top or tip joint of the index finger. Place the thumb over the pick. Press lightly but firmly while keeping the thumb rigid (fig. 6).

Rest the forearm on the edge of the guitar just above the bridge base (fig. 7).

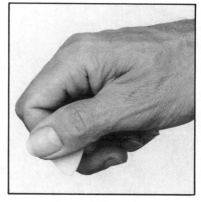
fig. 6 Holding the pick.

fig. 7 Forearm position.

There are three commonly-used hand positions: 1) free floating, 2) fanning the fingers, and 3) resting the palm of the hand on the strings behind the bridge. In the free-floating position, the middle, ring and little fingers are curled into the hand. They follow the movement of the thumb and index finger as the hand moves from string to string (fig. 1). Some guitarists fan the fingers and allow the little finger to skim the pick guard (fig. 2). For more stability or for special effects, the palm of the hand can lightly rest on the strings just behind the bridge (fig. 3).

fig. 1 Free-floating position.

fig. 2 Fanning the fingers.

fig. 3 Resting the palm.

The **DOWN-STROKE** (⊓) is the basic stroke used in pickstyle. In the *down-stroke*, the thumb pushes the pick through the string, stops short of the next string and immediately returns to the starting position. Use an economy of motion. Only follow through enough to finish picking the string. The angle of the pick to the strings should be fairly upright (fig. 4).

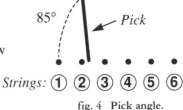

fig. 4 Pick angle.

An **UP-STROKE** (V) is generally used on the note that occurs between the beats, commonly called the upbeat (*an*). In playing the *up-stroke*, the index finger pushes the pick through the string. Use a minimum amount of movement. Follow through only enough to finish picking the string and then return to the starting point. Use *alternate down-* and *up-strokes* ⊓ V when playing a succession of eighth notes. Use the down-stroke on the downbeats and the up-stroke on the upbeats.

LEFT-HAND POSITION

An excellent way to develop a good **LEFT-HAND POSITION** is to begin by making a fist without bending the wrist. Now bring the hand up to the neck of the guitar and place the fingers on the fingerboard. The wrist should be straight, the fingers curved and the thumb should oppose the fingers in a "grip" position (fig. 5). Most guitarists find their maximum strength when their thumb opposes a spot located between the 1st and 2nd fingers.

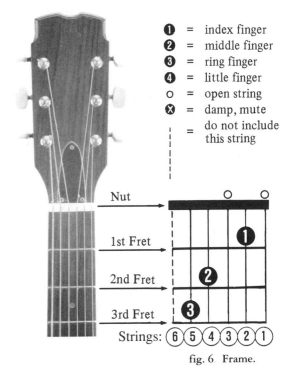

❶ = index finger
❷ = middle finger
❸ = ring finger
❹ = little finger
o = open string
⊗ = damp, mute
 = do not include this string

fig. 6 Frame.

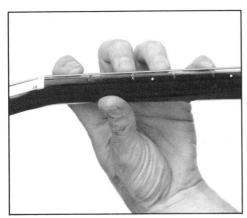

fig. 5 Finger position.

FRAMES are used by guitarists to indicate the placement of the *left-hand fingers* on the fingerboard (fig. 6). The numbers placed on or above the frame represent the fingers of the left hand. The letter O stands for an open string and an X means not to play the string.

Tuning the Guitar to Itself

The guitar can provide its own *tuning pitch*. Begin with the 6th string. Either tune it to a tuning pitch provided by some outside source (tuning fork, pitchpipe, piano, record) or estimate the pitch. The pitch of the low E, 6th string usually doesn't vary too much between tunings. Now proceed through the various steps described in steps 1–5.

1. Press 5th fret, 6th string to get the pitch for the open 5th string (A).

2. Press 5th fret, 5th string to get the pitch for the open 4th string (D).

3. Press 5th fret, 4th string to get the pitch for the open 3rd string (G).

4. Press 4th fret, 3rd string to get the pitch for the open 2nd string (B).

5. Press 5th fret, 2nd string to get the pitch for the open 1st string (E).

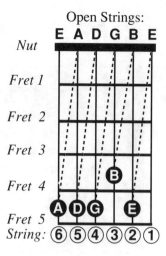

Tuning to a Piano

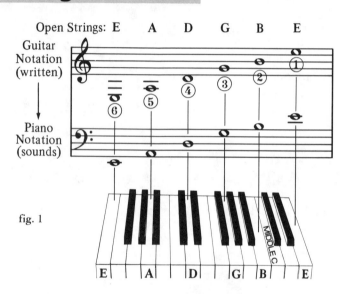

fig. 1

Guitar notation *sounds* an octave (eight notes) lower than written. So when you tune your guitar to a piano, you must be certain that you are tuning the strings to the correct pitch (fig. 1). Play the *tuning pitch* on the piano and then attempt to match the open guitar string to it. Begin with the 6th string.

Electronic Tuners

There are many inexpensive electronic guitar tuners available that will eliminate the tuning problem for you. They have built-in microphones for acoustic guitars and a cord input for electric guitars. They are well worth the investment.

MUSIC NOTATION

In music notation, **NOTES** are the basic symbols used to indicate rhythm. Rhythm refers to the duration, length, or time value given to a note. A quarter note generally represents the basic beat or pulse in music.

QUARTER NOTE. A quarter note receives one count or beat. It has a solid head with a stem attached to the side. Use your foot to *tap* the rhythm of the quarter note. Each note receives a *down* and an *up* (fig. 2).

HALF NOTE. A half note receives two counts or beats. It has an empty head with a stem attached to the side. Use your foot to *tap* the rhythm of the half note. Each note receives a *down-up-down-up* (fig. 3).

WHOLE NOTE. The whole note receives four counts or beats. This note does not have a stem. Use your foot to *tap* the rhythm of the whole note. Each note receives four *down-ups* (fig. 4).

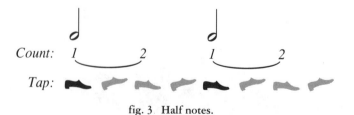

fig. 2 Quarter notes.

fig. 3 Half notes.

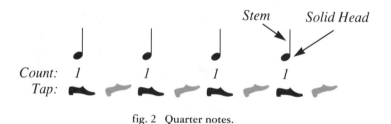

fig. 4 Whole notes.

Staff

Notes are placed on a **STAFF** to indicate their *pitch* or *sound*. Pitch refers to the relative high or lowness of a sound. The *staff* has five lines and four spaces (fig. 1). Notes can be placed on a line or in a space (fig. 2 and 3). The higher the note is placed on the staff, the higher the note sounds.

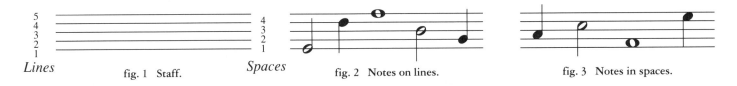

Lines   fig. 1 Staff.   Spaces   fig. 2 Notes on lines.   fig. 3 Notes in spaces.

Bar Lines, Measures and Time Signatures

BAR LINES are used to organize notes into **MEASURES** that have the same number of *beats* in them. The most common placement of bar lines is every four beats. A *double bar line* is used at the end of a song.

The 4/4 **TIME SIGNATURE** is the most common *time signature*. The top number indicates how many beats are in a measure. The bottom number tells you what kind of a note receives one beat. The time signature is placed at the beginning of the music. As you *tap* your foot, clap the following rhythm.

$\frac{4}{4}$ = Four beats in each measure
$\frac{4}{4}$ = A quarter note receives one beat

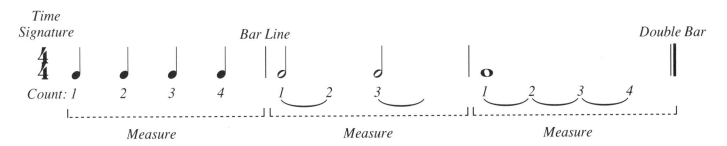

Time Signature   Bar Line   Double Bar

Count: 1   2   3   4   1   2   3   1   2   3   4

Measure   Measure   Measure

Clef Sign

A **CLEF SIGN** is added to the music staff to indicate what the notes on the lines and spaces represent. Guitar notation uses a **TREBLE** or **G CLEF** (fig. 4). The 1st seven letters of the alphabet are used to give names to the notes—A, B, C, D, E, F, G. The names of the lines are E, G, B, D, F—Every Good Boy Does Fine. The names of the spaces are F, A, C, E which spells **FACE**.

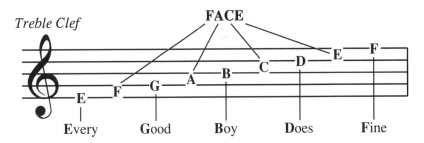

fig. 4 The treble clef and names of lines and spaces.

Tablature

TABLATURE is a six line staff that graphically represents the guitar fingerboard. Numbers placed on the tablature represent the frets of the guitar. The *fret* and *string* of any note can be indicated by placing a number on the appropriate line of the tablature. Tablature is a system of notation often used in rock, country, folk and blues styles of guitar playing (fig. 5).

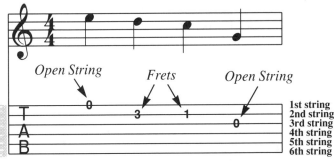

fig. 5 Tablature.

NOTES ON THE FIRST STRING

E Open, 1st string

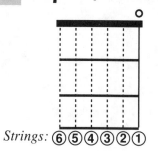

Strings: ⑥⑤④③②①

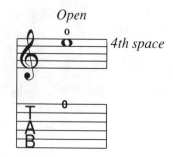

Open

4th space

The 1st string of the guitar is the highest sounding and thinnest string. As you hold the guitar, it is the string nearest the floor. In music notation, the **OPEN E, 1ST STRING** is located on the 4th space of the staff. "Open" means the string is not fingered.

Before playing exercises 1–4, it will be helpful to review and practice the **PICKSTYLE** right-hand techniques presented on page 4. Use a *down-stroke* (⊓) on each note.

1.
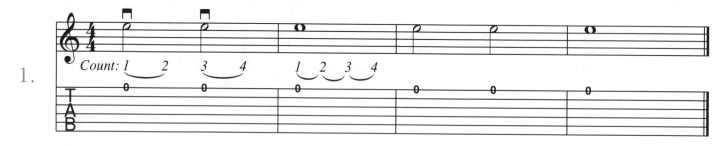

Count: 1   2   3   4   1   2   3   4

2.
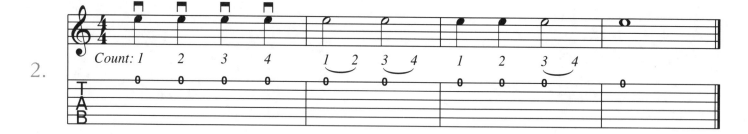

Count: 1   2   3   4   1   2   3   4   1   2   3   4

F 1st fret, 1st string

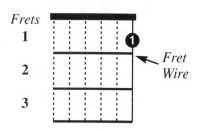

Frets
1
2
3

Fret Wire

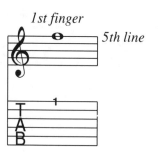

1st finger

5th line

Place the 1st finger of the left hand on the 1st fret as close as possible to the fret wire. The fleshy part of the finger should be actually touching the fret wire. Apply pressure just behind the fret wire. In music notation, the F is located on the 5th line of the music staff.

3.

Count: 1   2   3   4

4.

MIST

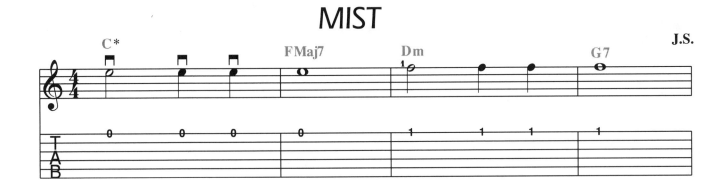

J.S.

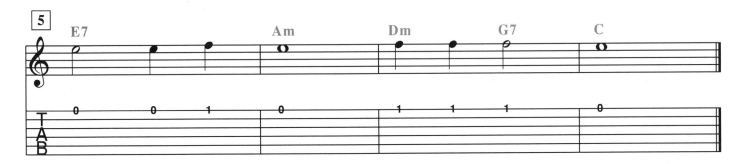

5

*The gray letters placed above the music indicate chords that can be played by another guitarist.

G 3rd fret, 1st string

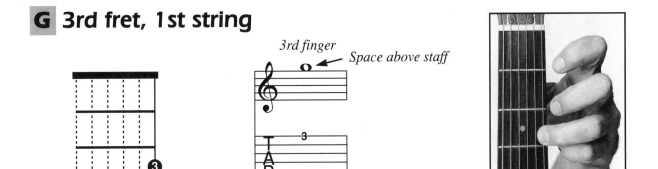

3rd finger

Space above staff

Place the 3rd or ring finger of the left hand on the 3rd fret immediately behind the fret wire. Keep the left hand fingers *spread apart* so that the index finger is above the 1st fret. In music notation, the G is located on the 1st space above the staff.

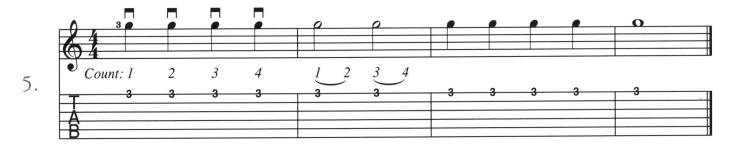

5.

6.

REVIEW: Notes on the 1st String: E, F and G

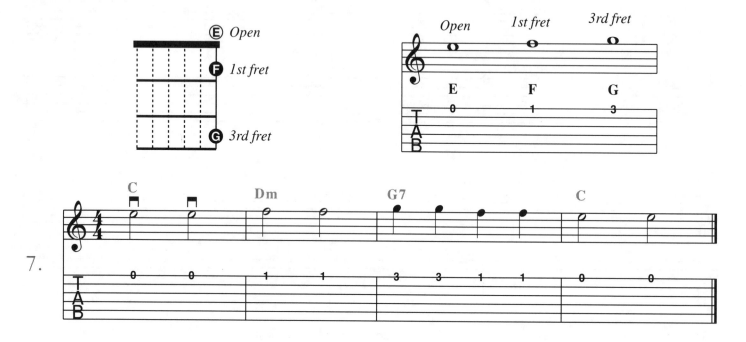

7.

Play the notes using a down-stroke (⊓) with the pick. The down-stroke (⊓) will be eliminated from this point on unless it is needed to help clarify the right-hand technique

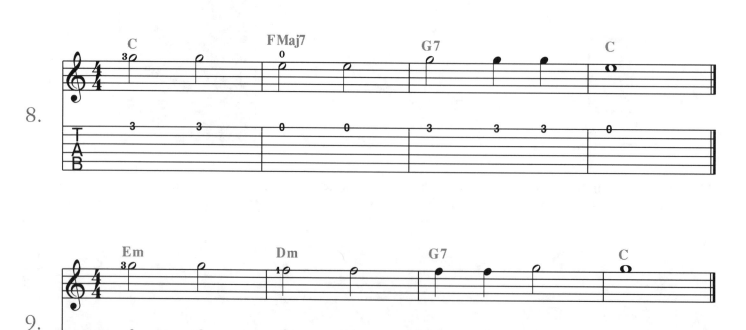

8.

9.

Chelsie uses the 1st string notes E, F and G. Play the melody as your teacher or friend plays a chord accompaniment. Play the song at a slow tempo (speed). Keep a steady beat.

CHELSIE

J.S.

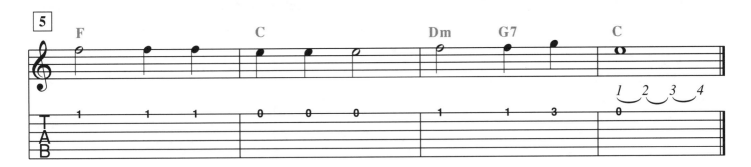

NOTES ON THE SECOND STRING

B **Open, 2nd string**

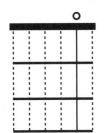

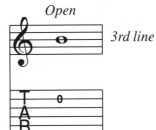

Open

3rd line

The open 2nd string is tuned to B. In music notation, the B is located on the 3rd or middle line of the music staff.

10.

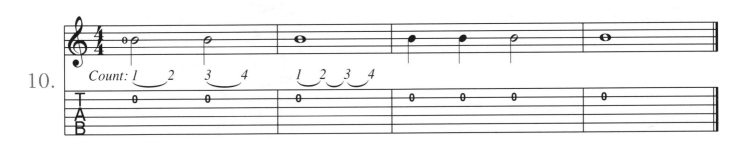

11.

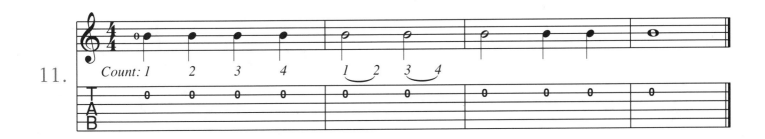

C 1st fret, 2nd string

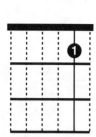

1st finger

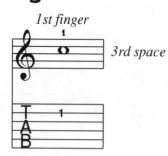

3rd space

Place the index finger of the left hand on the 1st fret, 2nd string, just behind the metal fret. In music notation, the C is located in the 3rd space of the staff.

12.

Count: 1 2 3 4 1 2 3 4

B-C MIX

G   Am   D7   G

D 3rd fret, 2nd string

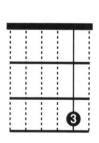

3rd finger

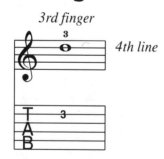

4th line

Place the 3rd finger of the left hand on the 3rd fret of the 2nd string. D is located on the 4th line of the music staff.

13.

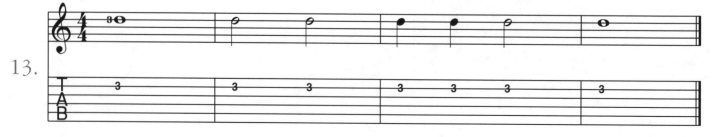

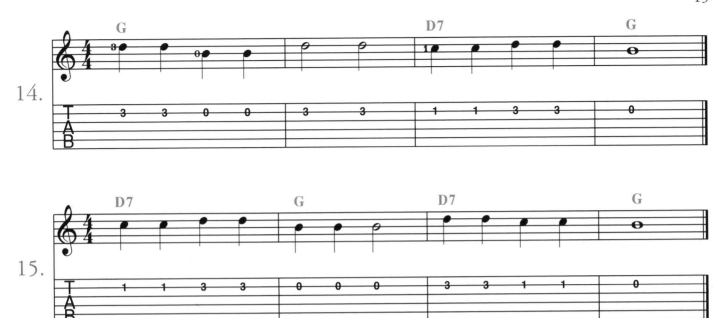

REVIEW: Notes on the 1st and 2nd Strings

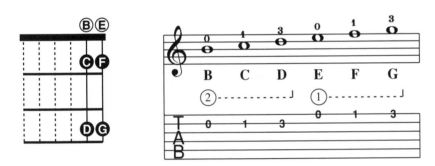

Notice that the left-hand fingering pattern is the same for both the 1st and 2nd strings. Keep the fingers spread above the frets. The thumb is placed on the back of the neck at a spot that opposes the 1st and 2nd fingers (see page 5).

Tempo Markings

TEMPO refers to the speed of the music. Three principal tempo markings are *Andante* (slow), *Moderato* (moderately) and *Allegro* (fast).

EASY ROCK

J.S.

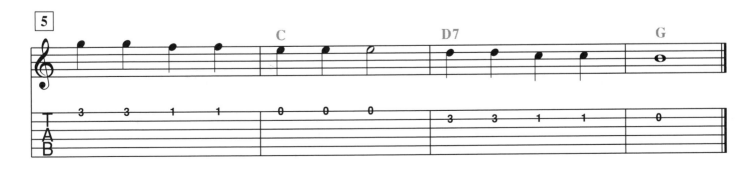

ROCKIN' ON TWO

BREEZIN'

Quarter Rest

A rest is a symbol used in music to indicate *silence*. For each note, there is a corresponding rest that has the same time value. A *quarter rest* receives one count or beat. Rests are counted the same way you count notes. A parenthesis placed around the count number indicates a rest.

Count: (1)

Tap:

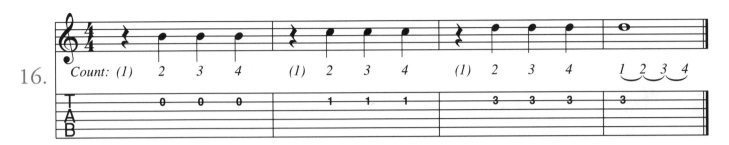

Repeat Sign

REPEAT SIGNS are used in music to avoid writing out repeated passages of music. The sign consists of a double bar with two dots on the inside of the *first* measure to be repeated and another double bar with two dots on the inside of the *last* measure to be repeated. Play all the measures inside the repeat signs twice.

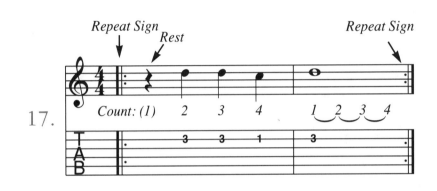

COMIN' OUT ROCK

J.S.

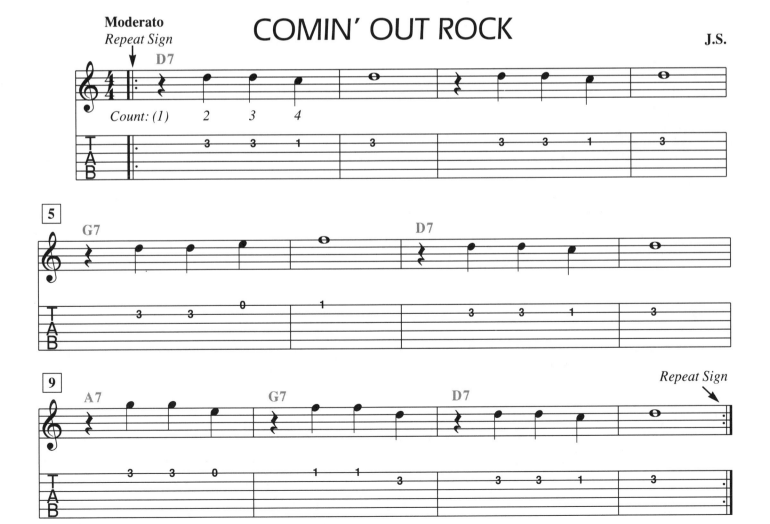

Dotted Half Note

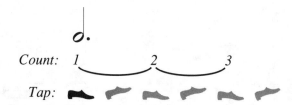

Count: 1   2   3

Tap:

A **DOT** increases the value of the note it is added to by one half. A dotted half note receives three counts or beats (2 + 1). Count and tap the beats as you play.

3/4 Time Signature

The 3/4 **TIME SIGNATURE** organizes the music into three beats per measure. The first beat of the measure should receive more emphasis or stress. Count: 1 2 3 | 1 2 3.

3 = Three beats in each measure
4 = A quarter note receives one beat

SORT OF BLUE

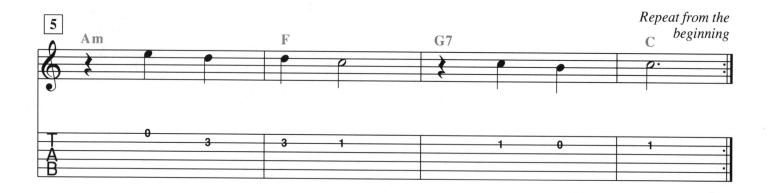

Tie

A **TIE** is a curved line that connects two notes of the *same pitch*. A tie is necessary if you wish to add the value of two notes together. Play the first note and hold it for the combined count of two notes.

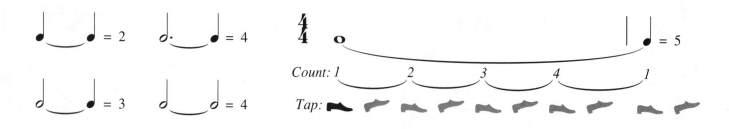

SOME KIND OF SUNSET

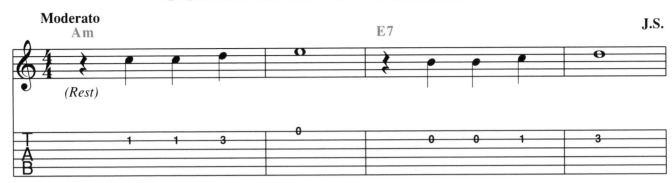

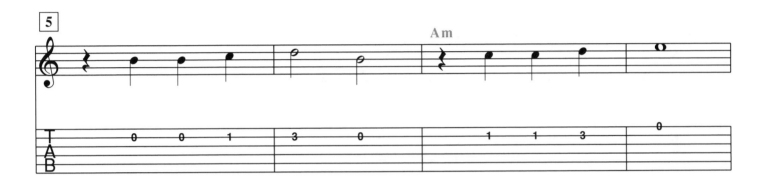

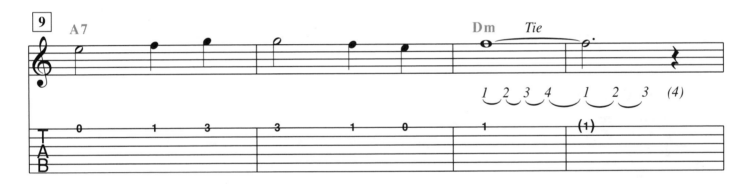

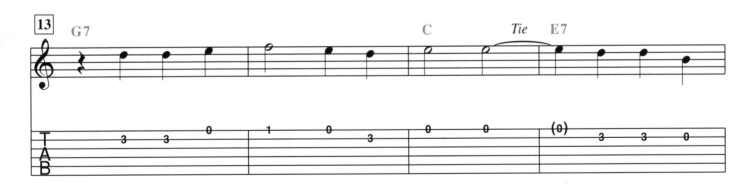

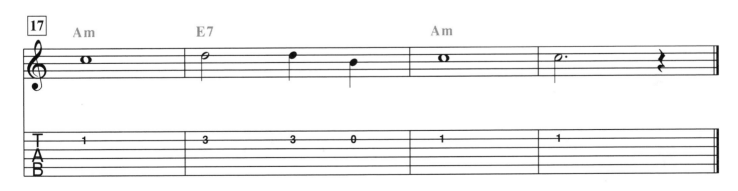

18

NOTES ON THE THIRD STRING

G Open, 3rd string

The open 3rd string is G. It is located on the 2nd line of the music staff. When a stem is added to a G, it is attached to the right side and extends above the note head.

A 2nd fret, 3rd string

Place the 2nd finger of the left hand on the 2nd fret, 3rd string. In music notation, the A is located on the 2nd space of the music staff.

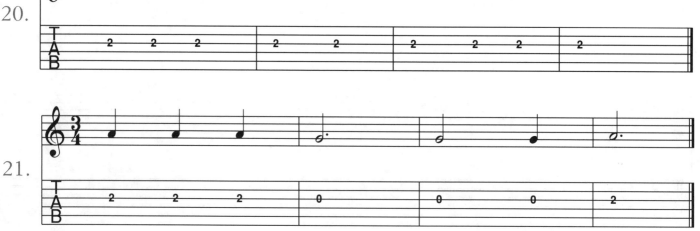

REVIEW: Notes on the 1st, 2nd and 3rd Strings

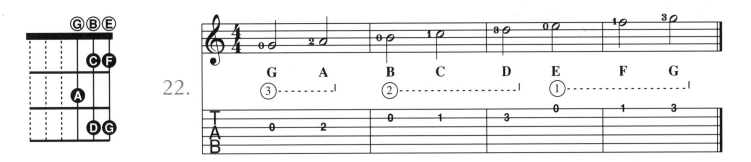

22.

FIRST and SECOND ENDINGS are another way of directing the player to repeat a section of music. In *Jingle Bells,* play the 1st two lines of music and the *1st ending* up to the repeat sign. Go back to the beginning and repeat the 1st and 2nd lines of music. Skip the 1st ending and play the *2nd ending.*

JINGLE BELLS

J. Pierpont

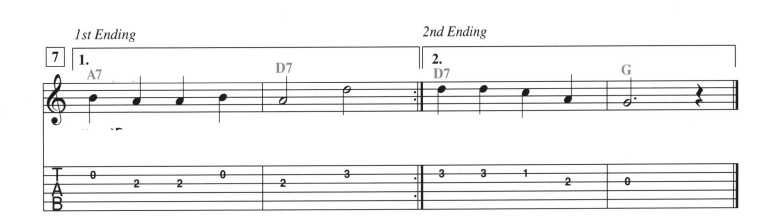

CHORDS

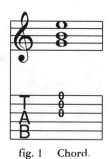

fig. 1   Chord.

When three or more notes are played at the *same time*, it is called a **CHORD**. The notes are placed above and below each other on the music staff and are played simultaneously (fig. 1).

Strum Techniques

The **STRUM TECHNIQUE** is the easiest to use when you are just beginning to learn how to play chords. Using one of the techniques described below, strum the open 3rd string and then continue *downward* across the 2nd and 1st strings (fig. 2).

fig. 2   Strum technique.

PICKSTYLE. Strum the strings with a *pick* held between your thumb and index finger. Review page 4. Use a *down-stroke* (⊓) as you strum from the 3rd string toward the 1st string (fig. 3 and 4). In the down-stroke, the thumb *pushes* the pick through the strings. When you have completed the strum, return your hand to the starting position.

fig. 3   Pickstyle preparation.

fig. 4   Completion.

Em Chord 3 strings

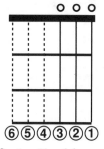

fig. 5   Chord frame.

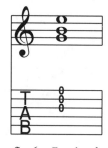

fig. 6   Em chord.

The **E minor (Em) CHORD** can be played by strumming or plucking the open 3rd, 2nd, and 1st strings of the guitar. A chord frame is often used to notate guitar chords (fig. 5). Dashed lines mean that these strings are omitted from the chord. The letter O stands for *open string* (review page 9). The Em chord is notated in standard music notation in figure 6.

23.

C and G⁷ Chords 3 strings

Two additional chords that can be played on the treble strings (strings 3, 2 and 1) are the **C CHORD** and the **G SEVENTH (G7) CHORD**.

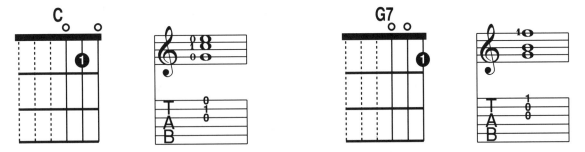

To play the C chord, place the tip of the left-hand index finger on the 1st fret, 2nd string. Make certain that you are not touching the 1st or 3rd string. For the G7 chord, depress the 1st string at the 1st fret with the index finger. Practice the following exercise.

CHORD STUDY

G Chord 3 strings

To play this **G CHORD**, fret the 1st string at the 3rd fret. Use the 3rd or ring finger of the left hand. Strum or pluck the 3rd, 2nd and 1st strings.

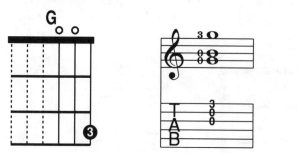

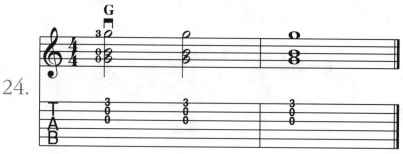

24.

Da Capo (D.C.) al Fine

DA CAPO or **D.C.** means "from the beginning." It directs the player to go back to the beginning of the music. *D.C. al Fine* directs the player to return to the beginning of the music and to play until reaching the place marked *Fine* (end). In *Meditation*, play the 1st line of music and then repeat it (at the repeat sign). Then continue on and play the 2nd line of music. Observe the *D.C. al Fine* and go back to the beginning of the music. Play the 1st line of music again and end at the *Fine* (at the end of the 1st line).

MEDITATION

Half Step and Whole Step

The distance between two tones is called an *interval*. The smallest interval is the **HALF STEP**. Guitar frets are placed a *half step* apart on the fingerboard. In the musical alphabet—A, B, C, D, E, F, G—there are two *natural half steps*. They occur between B and C (fig. 1) and E and F (fig. 2).

Two half steps (½ + ½) equal a **WHOLE STEP**. All of the other tones in the musical alphabet are a *natural whole step* apart. For example, the interval distance between C and D (fig. 3) and F and G (fig. 4) is a *whole step*. These notes are two frets apart.

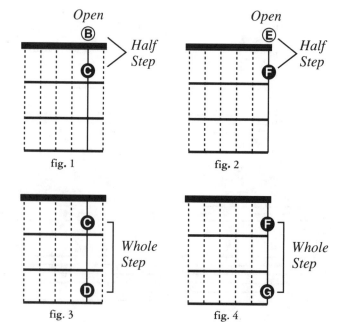

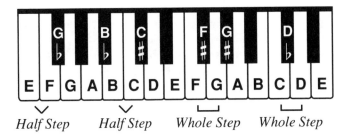

fig. 1 Piano keyboard.

Notes located between the natural whole steps are called **SHARPS** (♯) or **FLATS** (♭). On the piano keyboard, the black keys are sharps or flats (fig. 1). On the guitar, the notes that occur between the natural whole steps are the sharps or flats.

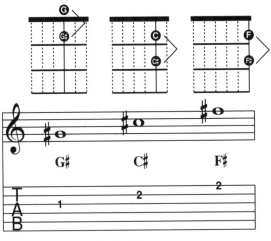

Sharps

When a **SHARP** (♯) is placed before a note in music notation, it *raises* the note one half step higher. On the guitar, that is the distance of one fret (fig. 2).

fig. 2 Sharps.

F♯ 2nd fret, 1st string

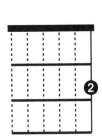 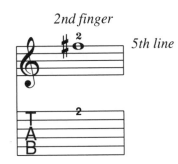 

Place the 2nd finger of the left hand on the 2nd fret, 1st string. The customary practice in music notation is to write the sharp once for each measure. All F's are to be played as F♯ until and up to the bar line. The bar line cancels the sharp so that it must be written in again if there are any F sharps to be played in the next measure. Play the following drill.

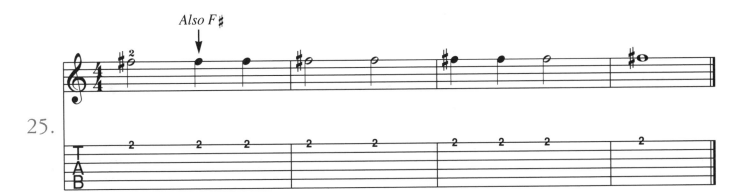

D⁷ Chord 3 strings

Arch the 2nd finger when playing the **D7 CHORD** to make certain that it is not touching the 2nd string. Place the fingers just behind the fret wire. If a fretted string does not produce a clear tone, you need to either press more firmly or move the finger closer to the fret wire. The left-hand fingernails must be short.

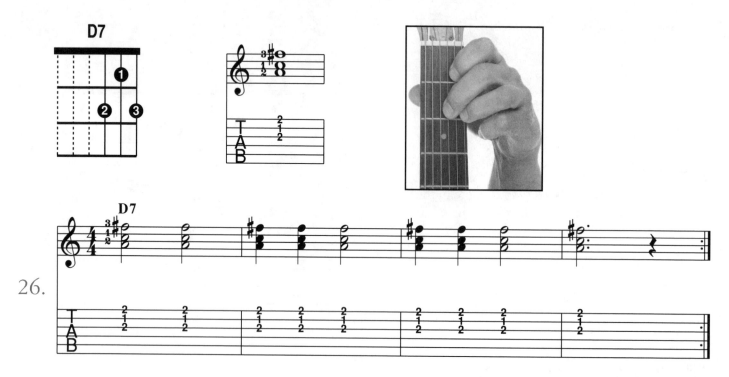

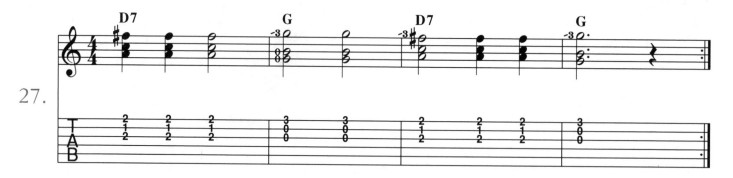

GUIDE FINGER. The 3rd finger (⌐3) serves as a *guide finger* when going from the D7 to G chord. It maintains contact with the 1st string as it *slides* from the 2nd to the 3rd fret. There should be no sound as the finger moves along the string. Also use this technique when going from the G to the D7 chord.

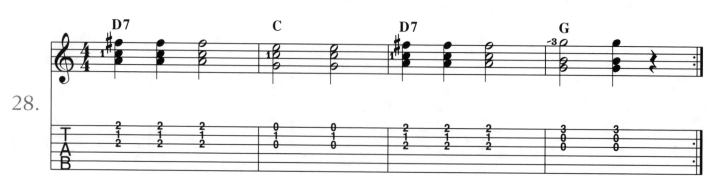

COMMON FINGER. The D7 and C chords have a *common finger*. In both chords, the 1st finger is on the 2nd string, 1st fret. Be sure to leave this finger down as you go from the D7 to the C chord.

MAJOR SCALE

A scale is a series of consecutive tones moving from one tone to another. The **MAJOR SCALE** is the most commonly used scale. The major scale is a series of eight successive tones that have a pattern of whole and half steps. The major scale has a half step between the 3rd and 4th tones and the 7th and 8th tones of the scale. All other scale tones are a whole step apart. In order to obtain the correct pattern of whole and half steps, an F# must be added to the **G MAJOR SCALE** (fig. 1 and 2).

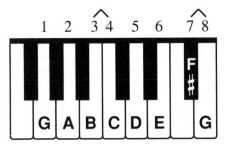

fig. 1 Keyboard analysis—G major scale.

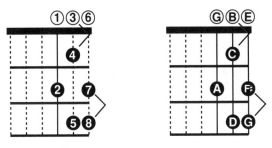

fig. 2 Fretboard analysis—G major scale.

Play the G major scale in exercise 29. Notice the *half steps* between the 3rd and 4th and the 7th and 8th tones of the scale. Then play the *G Scale Study*.

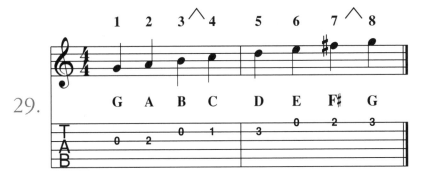

29.

G SCALE STUDY

Moderato

Dynamics

DYNAMICS are signs that indicate how loud or soft to play the music. They add interest to the music by adding contrast.

piano	(*p*)	Soft
mezzo piano	(*mp*)	Moderately Soft
mezzo forte	(*mf*)	Moderately Loud
forte	(*f*)	Loud
fortissimo	(*ff*)	Very Loud

Key Signature

A song based on the G major scale is in the **KEY OF G MAJOR**. Since the F is sharp in the G scale, every F will be sharp in the key of G major. Instead of individually sharping all the F's in the song, the sharp is indicated at the beginning of each line of music, in the **KEY SIGNATURE**. Sharps or flats shown in the key signature are effective throughout the song.

Principal Chords

The **PRINCIPAL CHORDS** are chords built on the 1st (I), 4th (IV), and 5th (V) tones of the major scale. In the key of G Major, the principal chords are G, C, and D7. The G chord functions as *home base*. Most songs in the key of G begin and end on a G chord. The D7 is the next most frequently used chord.

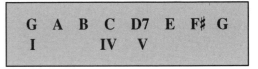

G	A	B	C	D7	E	F♯	G
I			IV	V			

Principal chords in G major

BASS CHORD STUDY

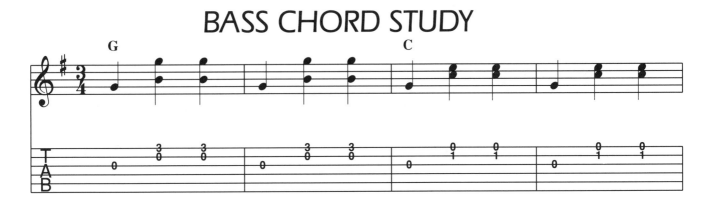

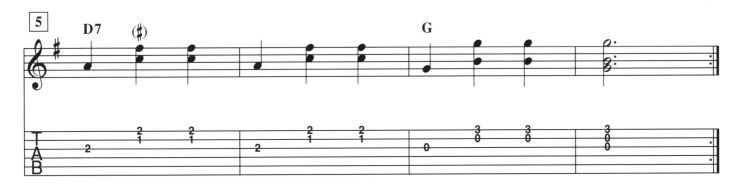

G♯ 4th fret, 1st string

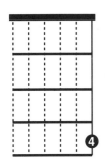

4th finger

Place the 4th finger (pinky) on the 4th fret, 1st string for the G♯. Remember that the sharp only needs to be written once in each measure.

30.

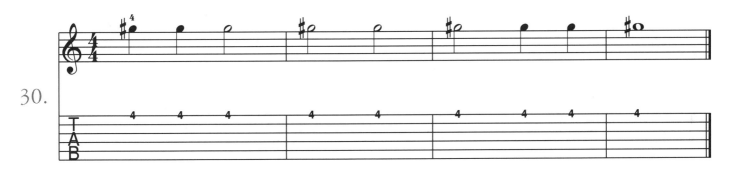

Natural Sign

A NATURAL SIGN (♮) is used to *cancel* the effect of a sharp or flat. When placed before a note, it returns the note to its natural or unaltered form.

31.

Leger Lines

LEGER LINES are lines that are added above or below the staff to extend its range. In order to notate the A, 5th fret, 1st string, it is necessary to add one leger line above the staff.

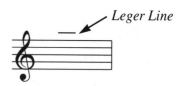

Leger Line

A 5th fret, 1st string

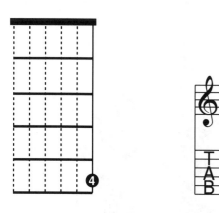

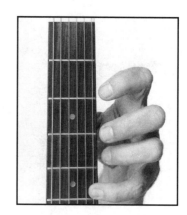

4th finger

In music notation, the A, 5th fret, 1st string is located on the 1st leger line above the staff. Shift the left hand, 4th finger up to the 5th fret. You are now in *2nd position*. It is called 2nd position because the 1st finger is at the 2nd fret.

32.

Shifting

The following exercise gives you some practice in **SHIFTING** the left hand from *1st position* to *2nd position* and back again. *Harvest* requires a shift to the 2nd position in order to play the A at the 5th fret.

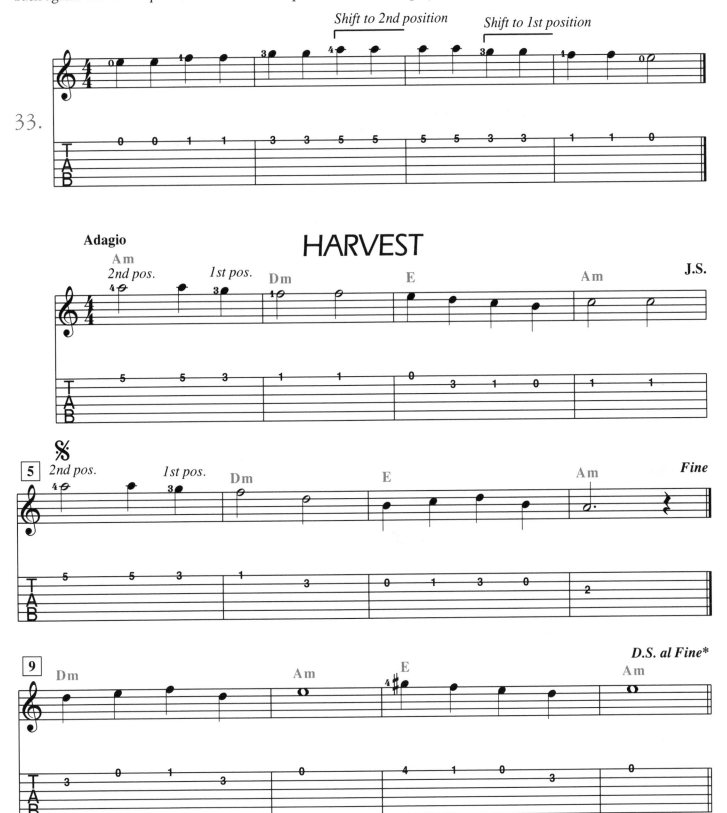

Dal Segno

*DAL SEGNO** or **D.S.** means "from the sign." It is one of the signs used in music that directs the player to skip back through the music to a place marked with a sign (𝄋). *D.S. al Fine* means to go back and play from the sign to the placed marked *Fine* (end). In this case, go back to the 2nd line and play it again.

Open Bass Strings

The 4th, 5th and 6th strings of the guitar are called the **BASS STRINGS**. The open 4th string is the **D** string. In music notation, it is located on the 1st space below the staff (fig. 1). The open 5th string is an **A**. In order to notate the A, two *leger lines* must be added below the staff. The A is located on the 2nd leger line (fig. 2). The 6th string or E string is the lowest note on the guitar. Three leger lines need to be added to the staff to notate E. The E is located on the space below the 3rd leger line (fig. 3).

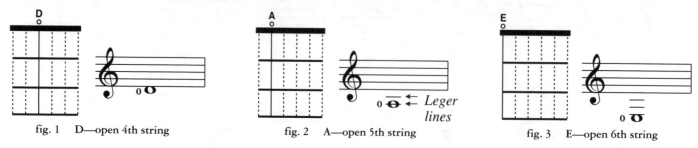

fig. 1   D—open 4th string   fig. 2   A—open 5th string   fig. 3   E—open 6th string

Use a *down-stroke* (⊓) with a **PICK**. Check your arm and hand positions. Be sure that your forearm is placed on the edge of the guitar just above the bridge base.

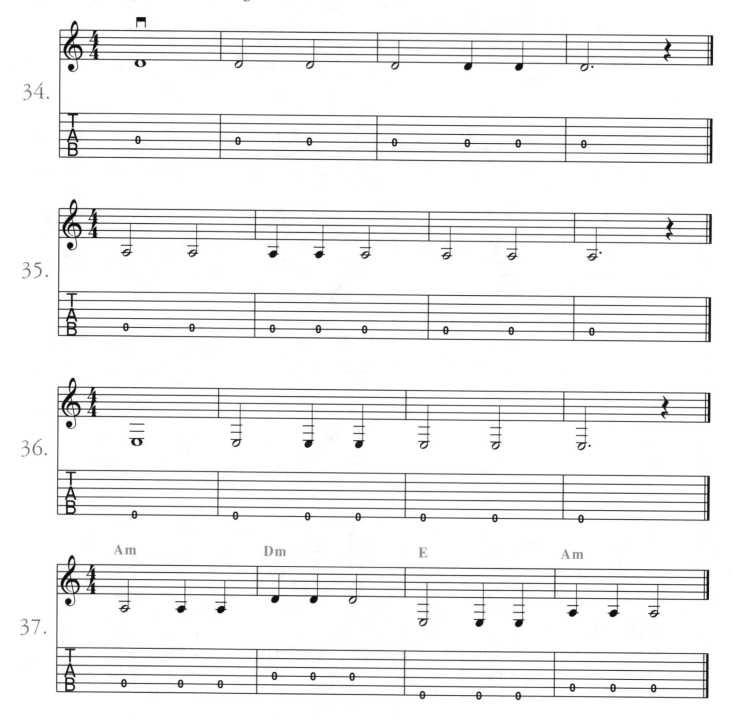

EIGHTH NOTES

Beam

Count: 1 an
Tap: down up

fig. 1 Eighth notes.

An **EIGHTH NOTE** receives one half of a count or beat. It can be played on the *down* or on the *up* part of the beat. Eighth notes are commonly played in pairs and are attached with a beam.

Eighth notes move twice as quickly as quarter notes. Count them by inserting the word "an" between the numbers. For example: 1 an 2 an 3 an 4 an (fig. 2).

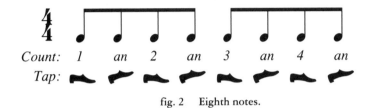

Count: 1 an 2 an 3 an 4 an
Tap:

fig. 2 Eighth notes.

PLAYING TECHNIQUES

Pickstyle. Use an *up-stroke* (V) with the pick on eighth notes that occur on the upbeat (an). In playing the *up-stroke*, the index finger pushes the pick through the string. Follow through only enough to finish picking the string and then return to the starting point. Remember to use a minimum of movement. Use *alternate down* and *up-strokes* (⊓ V) when you are playing a succession of eighth notes. Use the *down-stroke* (⊓) on the downbeats and the *up-stroke* (V) on the upbeats.

Practice the following exercises using the *pickstyle* technique. Play the rhythm patterns on various open and fretted strings.

In popular music language, *lead* has become a synonym for melody or solo. A lead guitar player plays the solo or melodic material in a song.

ROCKIN' OUT (lead)

Rhythm Guitar

Pickstyle. When strumming eighth note patterns, it is only necessary to strum the 1st and 2nd strings on the *up-stroke* (V).

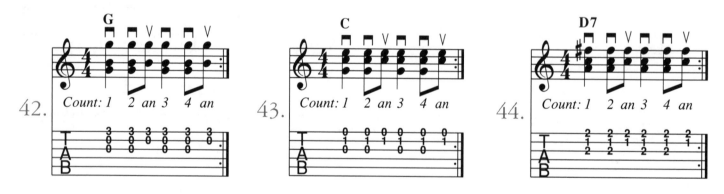

Practice the following rhythm patterns on the open 3rd, 2nd and 1st strings (Em chord). Count out loud as you strum. Tap your foot on the downbeats. Remember to play only the 1st and 2nd strings on the *up-strokes*.

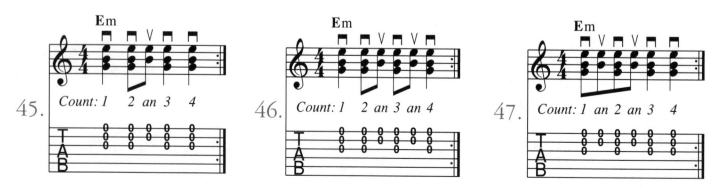

The following rhythm guitar part can be played with the lead line of *Rockin' Out*. If you do not have another guitarist to play with, use a tape recorder. A tape recorder can be a great aid in learning to play the guitar. Record the rhythm guitar part to *Rockin' Out* and practice the lead with your recording.

ROCKIN' OUT (rhythm)

J.S.

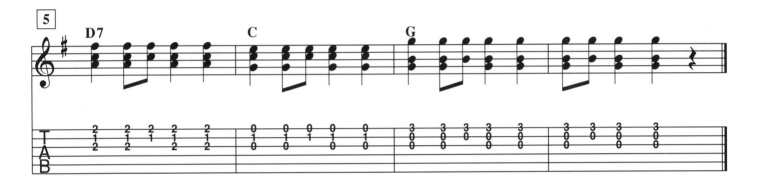

G and D⁷ Chords 4 strings

The open 4th string D can be added to the **G** and **D7** chords.

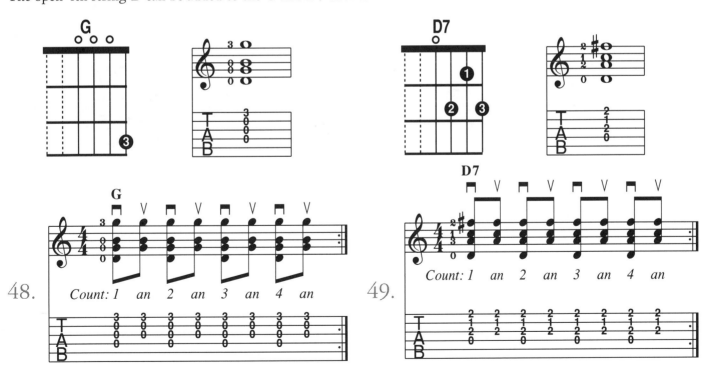

Rock rhythm patterns are developed from eighth-note rhythm patterns. It is important to learn how to play "straight eighths;" that is, eighth notes that are even, in strict tempo, and are exactly on the down and upbeats of the measure.

Pickstyle. Strum four down-strokes in the 1st measure and then start playing down- and up-strokes in the 2nd measure. Keep the rhythm even. When you play the up-stroke, it is only necessary to strum the 1st three strings (treble strings) with the pick. This technique makes the up-strokes lighter in sound than the down-strokes and helps to give you a more solid beat.

G JAM (rhythm)

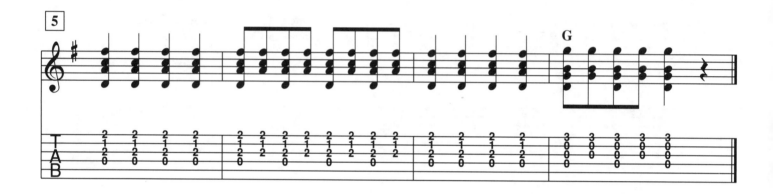

The following lead guitar part can be played with the rhythm part of *G Jam*.

G JAM (lead)

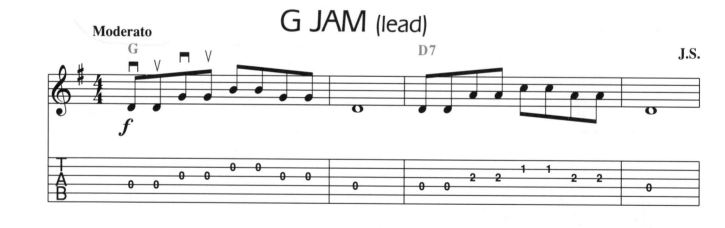

NOTES ON THE FOURTH STRING

E 2nd fret, 4th string

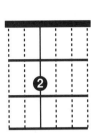
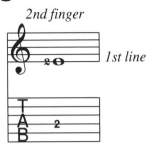

2nd finger

1st line

The **E** is located on the 4th string, 2nd fret. Use the 2nd finger to fret the note.

50.

51.

Em Chord 4 strings

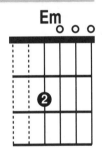
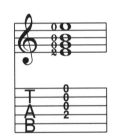

The E on the 4th string can be added to the **Em CHORD**. Keep the 2nd finger arched so that it does not touch the open 3rd string.

C Chord 4 strings

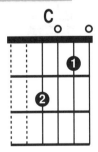
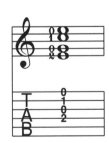

To play the **C Chord** (4 strings), place the middle finger on the 2nd fret, 4th string and the index finger on the 1st fret, 2nd string. Keep the fingers arched to avoid touching the open 3rd and 1st strings.

52.
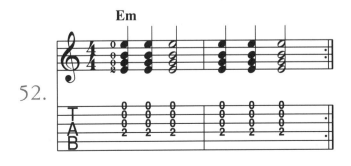

53.
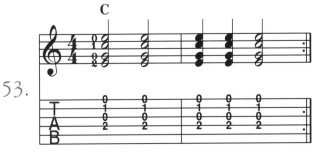

Rhythm Guitar

Review the G and D7 chords and then play the following exercise. Practice fingering the G chord with the 4th finger as well as with the 3rd finger.

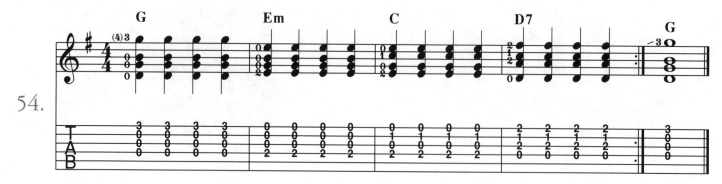

54.

Use alternating *down-up* strokes with a pick on the following exercise.

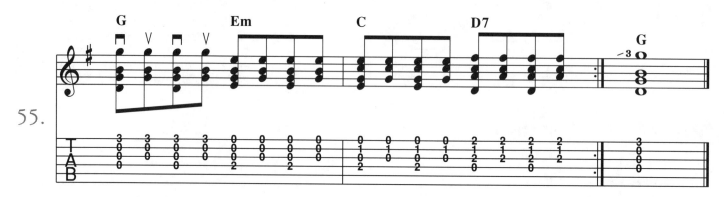

55.

In exercise 56, the 2nd upbeat (the *an* of 2) is TIED to the 3rd downbeat (3). Do not strum the chord on the 3rd downbeat. DROP the chord strum out of the pattern but *continue* the down-up *motion* of the pick. Just avoid strumming the strings on the 3rd downbeat. Give a little accent (>) or emphasis to the 2nd upbeat (the *an* of 2).

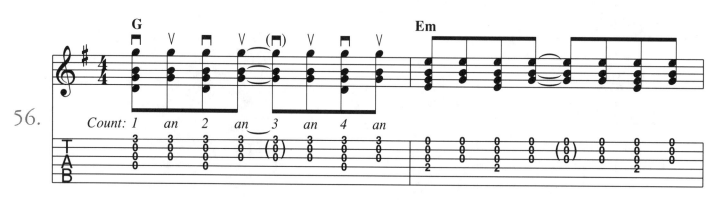

56.

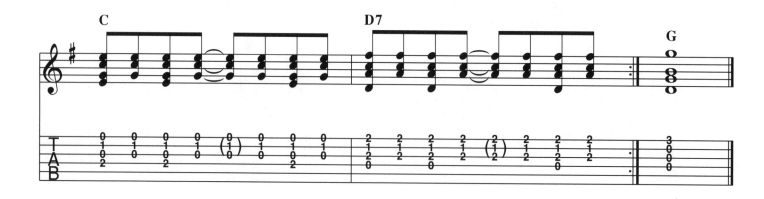

Lead Guitar

The following lead patterns or **RIFFS** (short melodies) can be played with exercises 54, 55 and 56. Have a friend or your teacher play the rhythm guitar chords as you play the lead patterns. Alternate the pick on the eighth notes. Use a down-stroke on the downbeats (numbered beats) and an up-stroke on the upbeats (an).

Bass-Chord Patterns: D⁷ and G⁷

Use a down-stroke with a pick on the open 4th string (D). Strum and accent (>) the chords on the 2nd and 4th downbeats of the measure. Notice that in exercise 63, you use two down-strokes on the eighth notes. The open D string has been added to the G7 chord (4 strings).

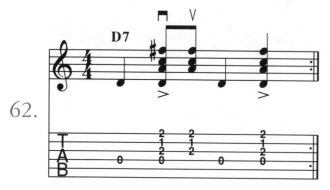

A⁷ Chord full

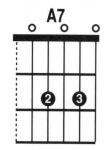

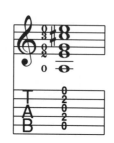

Bass-Chord Pattern: A⁷

The **A7 CHORD** has a C sharp (C♯) in it. The C♯ is located on the 2nd fret, 2nd string. Use the 2nd and 3rd fingers to fret this chord. This is the best fingering to use when going to the D7 chord.

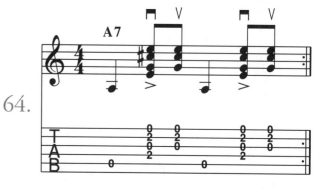

Before you attempt to play the rhythm guitar part for *Celebrate*, practice the chord progression, giving one down strum for each downbeat in the measure.

CELEBRATE (rhythm)

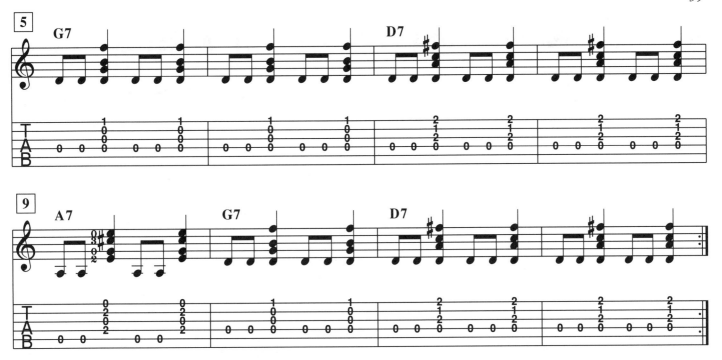

The following lead guitar part can be played with the rhythm guitar part of *Celebrate*.

CELEBRATE (lead)

Moderato

J.S.

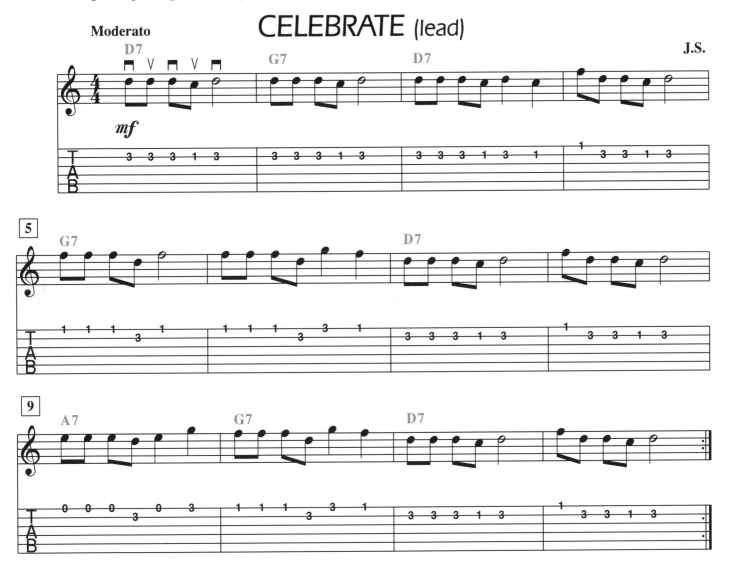

For additional practice in playing the G, C, G7 and A7 chords, play the chord changes to *Easy Rock* on page 13, *Comin' Out Rock* on page 15, and *Jingle Bells* on page 19. Record the melodies of these songs and play the chords with your recording. Begin by playing a chord on each beat in the measure.

ARPEGGIOS (broken chords)

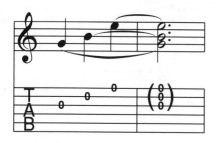

An **ARPEGGIO** is a *broken chord*. Individual notes of the chord are picked or plucked and are allowed to *sustain* or *ring* into the next note. This produces the sound of a chord though it is played only one note at a time.

PLAYING TECHNIQUE

Pickstyle. There is essentially no new technique to learn. Other than the fact that you will be changing from one string to another more frequently, the pickstyle technique of down-strokes on the downbeats and up-strokes on the upbeats remains the same.

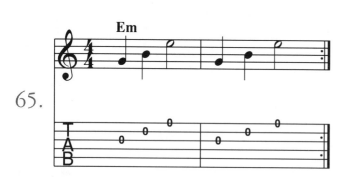

Am and E Chords 3 strings

To play the **A minor (Am) CHORD**, the fingers must be arched and *almost* on the tips to avoid touching adjacent strings. Keep your left hand fingernails short. The **E CHORD** contains a **G sharp**. The G♯ is located on the 1st fret, 3rd string.

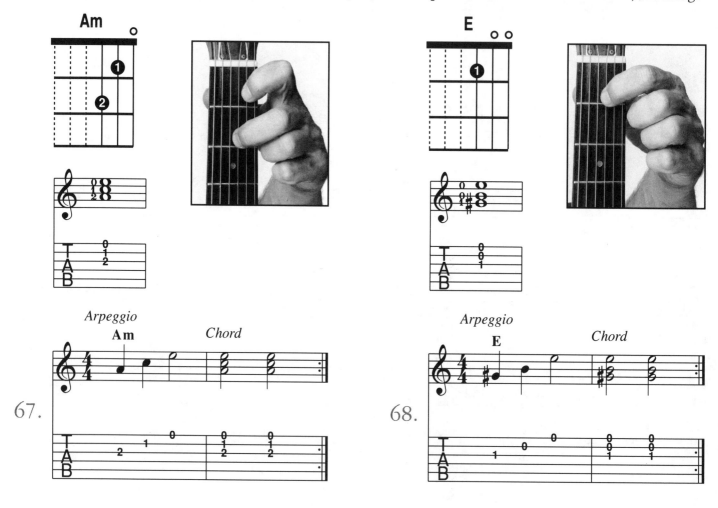

CHORD STUDY

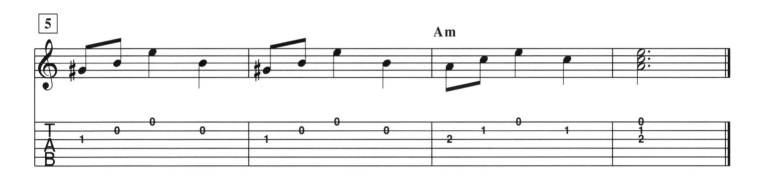

DAYBREAK (accompaniment)

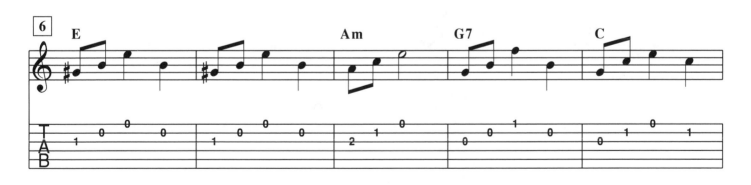

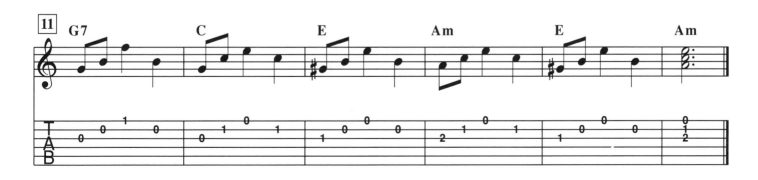

DAYBREAK (lead)

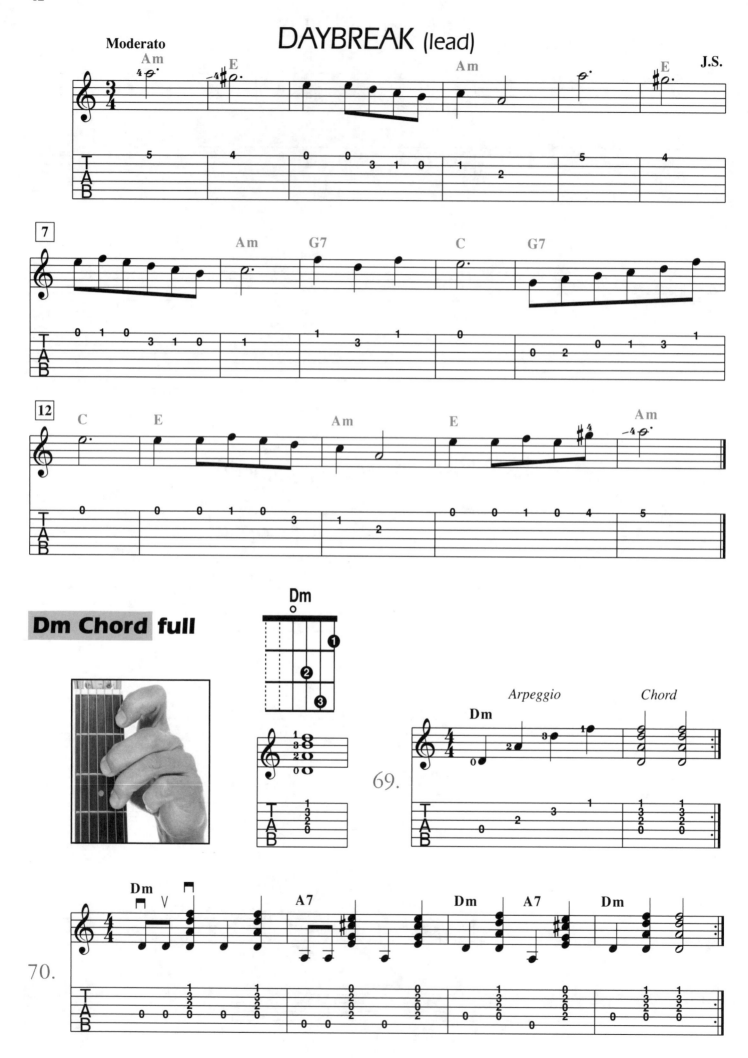

Dm Chord full

69.

70.

F 3rd fret, 4th string

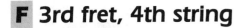
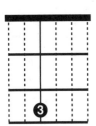
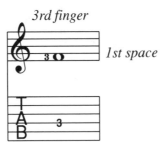

3rd finger

1st space

71.

Incomplete Measure

Songs do not always start on the 1st beat of the measure—they can begin on any beat. When this occurs it results in an **INCOMPLETE MEASURE** at the beginning and at the end of the song.

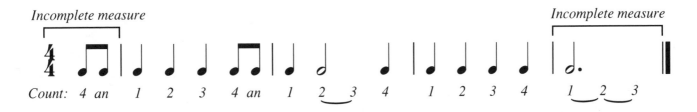

Incomplete measure

Incomplete measure

Count: 4 an   1   2   3   4 an   1   2   3   4   1   2   3   4   1   2   3

Moderato

SAINT JAMES INFIRMARY

Incomplete measure

Traditional

mf

Incomplete measure

Flats

A **FLAT** (♭) placed before a note *lowers* the note one half step. If the note is *fingered* (not an open string), play the next lower note or fret (fig. 1). If the note is located on an *open* string, play the 4th fret of the next lower string unless the string is the 3rd string, in which case you play the 3rd fret (fig. 2).

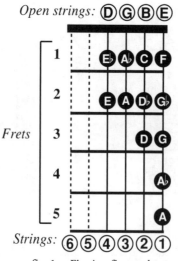

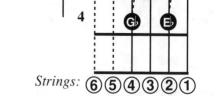

fig. 1 Flatting fingered notes.

fig. 2 Flatting open string notes.

Enharmonics. This is the term used to describe tones that actually sound one and the same, but are *named* and *written* differently. For example, D♯ and E♭ are the same tone even though they are written differently.

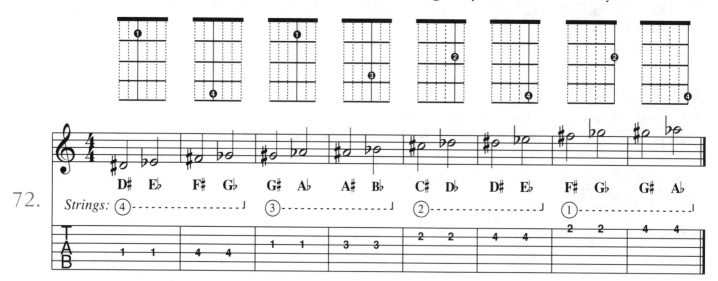

Chromatic Scale

A **CHROMATIC SCALE** is a scale in which each successive note is a *half step* apart (see page 30). Exercise 73 is the **G Chromatic Scale.** It begins on the open G, 3rd string and moves by half steps up to the G, 1st string, 3rd fret. Sharps (♯) are used on the ascending chromatic scale and flats (♭) are used when the scale descends.

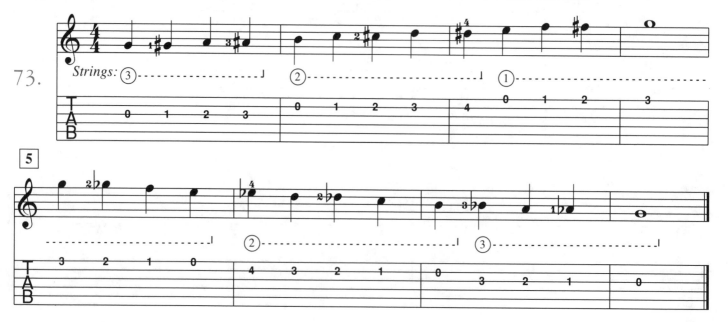

Tied Eighth-Note Rhythms

As you have learned, a **TIE** is used to connect two notes of the *same pitch* (see page 18). When a tie is used with quarter, half or whole notes, it generally extends the note value across the bar line into the next measure. The tie is also used within the same measure to tie eighth notes that occur on the upbeat (*an*) to a following quarter or half note. This results in rhythms that are commonly found in pop, jazz and rock music.

Syncopation. In 4/4 time, the normal accent (>) is on the 1st beat of the measure with the secondary accent on the 3rd beat (ex. 74). To accent a note means to stress one tone over others. When the accent is shifted to a normally weak beat, it is called *syncopation* (ex. 75). Play these two exercises on the open 1st string (E). Play the accented note a little louder.

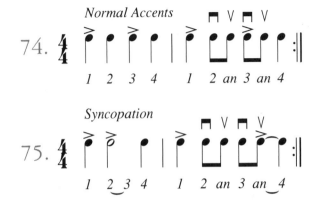

The tied eighth-note rhythms found in *Groovin'* are examples of syncopation. In preparation for playing the solo part, practice the following rhythm exercises on the open 1st string (E).

Groovin' contains two FLATS: A♭ on the 1st string in measure 4 and A♭ on the 3rd string in measure 8. You have previously played those notes as their *enharmonic* equivalent—G♯.

GROOVIN' (lead)

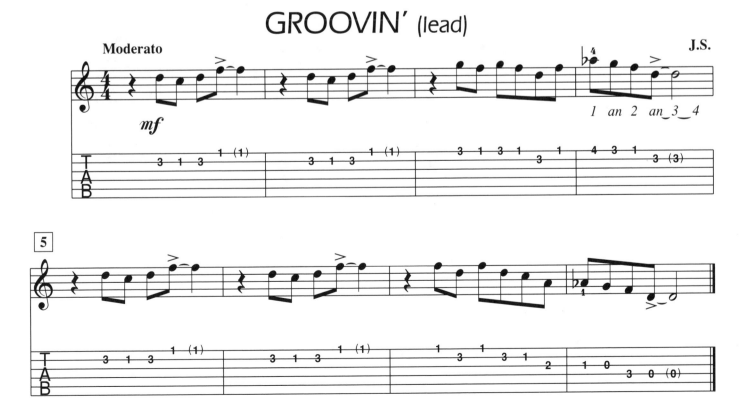

Rock rhythms are often based on a down-stroke motion. Play the accompaniment bass line to *Groovin'* using successive down-strokes with a pick. Slightly **MUTE** the strings by allowing the heel of the right hand to rest on the strings at the bridge. This will give you a "chucking" sound.

GROOVIN' (rhythm-bass)

J.S.

NOTES ON THE 5TH STRING

The **OPEN A, 5TH STRING** was introduced on page 30. **B** is located on the 2nd fret of this string and is fingered with the 2nd finger. **C** is located on the 3rd fret. Use the 3rd finger to fret this note.

Practice exercises 78 and 79 using a down-stroke with a pick.

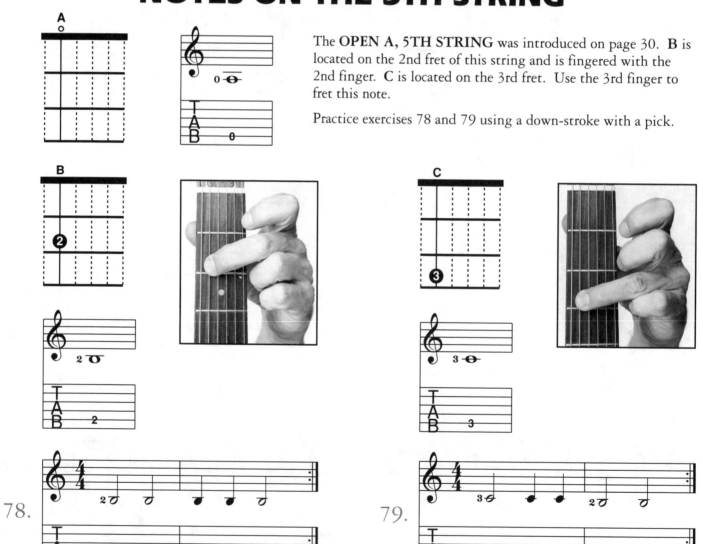

78.

79.

Shout has a rhythm-bass line that is similar to the one used in *Groovin'* except that it starts on the A, open 5th string. Use successive down-strokes with a pick and *mute* the strings with the heel of the right hand (see page 46).

SHOUT (rhythm-bass)

J.S.

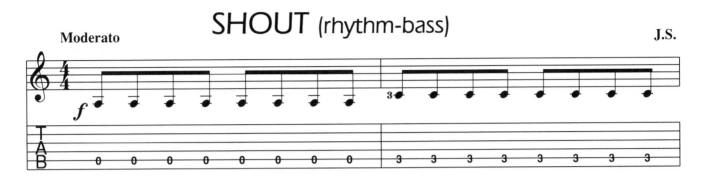

When you have learned the rhythm-bass part to *Shout*, make a recording of it. Practice the lead line with your recording. Keep it at a slow tempo until you can play the lead line without any hesitation or errors.

SHOUT (lead)

J.S.

Power Chords
rhythm guitar

The **A5**, **D5** and **E5** rock **POWER CHORDS** can be used for the rhythm-bass part of *Shout*. Each chord is a two-note chord. Use the index finger to fret the string as well as to dampen (**⊗**) the adjacent (higher in pitch) strings. The most effective playing technique is to use successive down-strokes with a pick as you *mute* the strings with the heel of your hand.

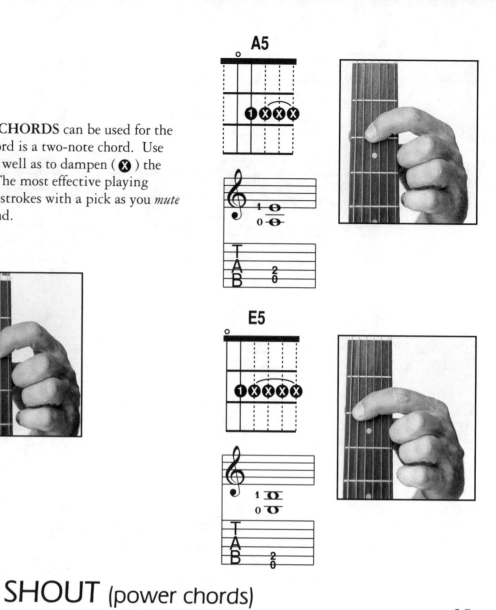

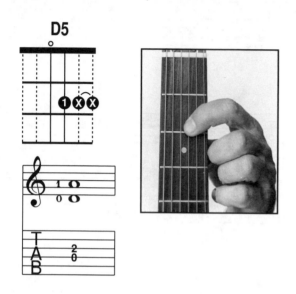

SHOUT (power chords)

A Chromatic Scale

The **A Chromatic Scale** moves by half steps from the open A, 5th string up to the A on the 3rd string, 2nd fret.

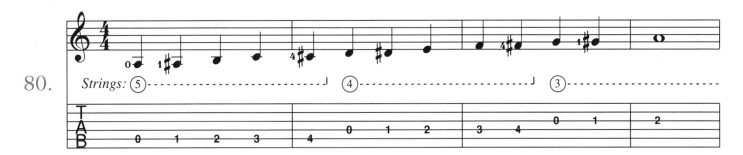

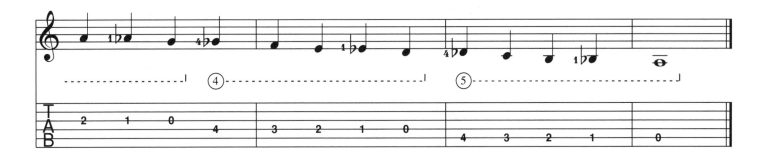

Chord/Bass Note Em/D

To indicate the *lowest* note of a chord, a slash (/) and the name of the note can be added after the chord name. For example, Em/D means to play an Em chord with a D in the bass. *Nuage* contains several examples of this chord/bass notation. This song also provides you with additional practice in playing sharps.

Natural Signs (♮). Natural signs are used to cancel or eliminate sharps and flats. The *bar line* also cancels sharps or flats that may have been added to the previous measure. In measure 2 of *Nuage*, the natural sign is added as a reminder. It is placed in parenthesis because the bar line has already canceled the D♯ that was added in measure 1.

NUAGE (chord study)

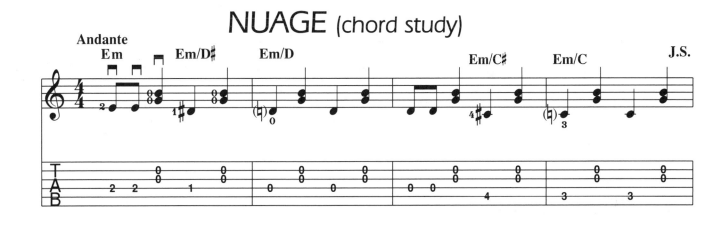

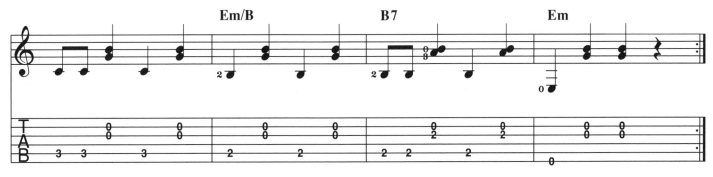

NOTES ON THE SIXTH STRING

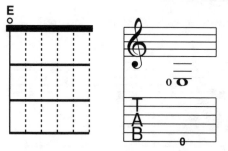

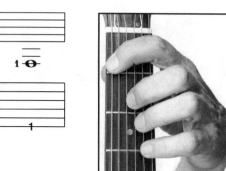

The **OPEN E, 6TH STRING** has been used in several songs and exercises since its introduction on page 30. Two additional notes on the 6th string are **F** and **G**. The F is located on the 1st fret and is fingered with the 1st finger. The G is located on the 3rd fret and is fingered with the 3rd finger.

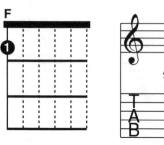

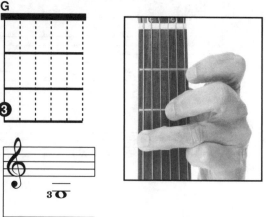

81.

82.

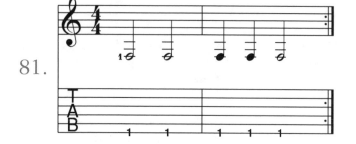

Am   Dm   G7   C

83.

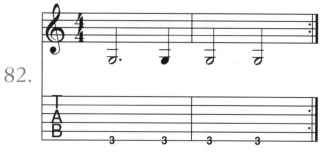

REVIEW: Bass Strings

84.

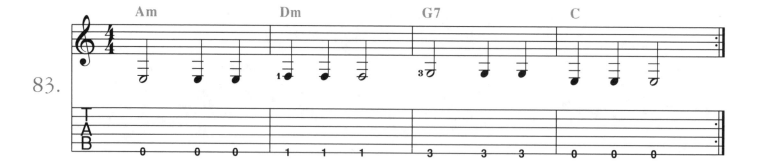

Walking Bass

A **WALKING BASS** line moves by step or by small skips from one chord tone to another. The rhythm is usually successive quarter notes; that is, one note for every beat in the measure.

85.

5

10
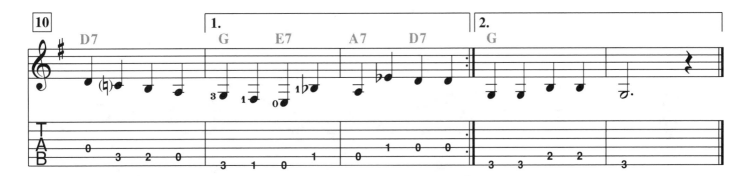

E⁷ Chord 4 strings

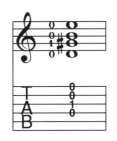

To play the **E7 CHORD,** place the tip of the index finger on the 1st fret, 3rd string. Strum or pluck the 4th, 3rd, 2nd and 1st strings. Practice exercise 86, then play the rhythm guitar part for the walking bass line presented above.

86.
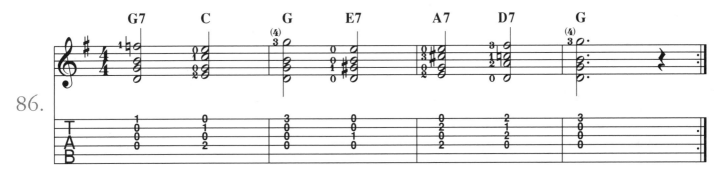

G Chord full

The full **G CHORD** has several common fingerings. You need to know them all. The fingering you use depends upon the chord that you are playing before and after the G chord. Figure 1 illustrates a good beginning G chord. Dampen (prevent from sounding) the open 5th string by lightly touching it with the finger that is fretting the 6th string. The G chords diagramed in figure 2 are optional fingerings. In these G chords, the 5th string is included.

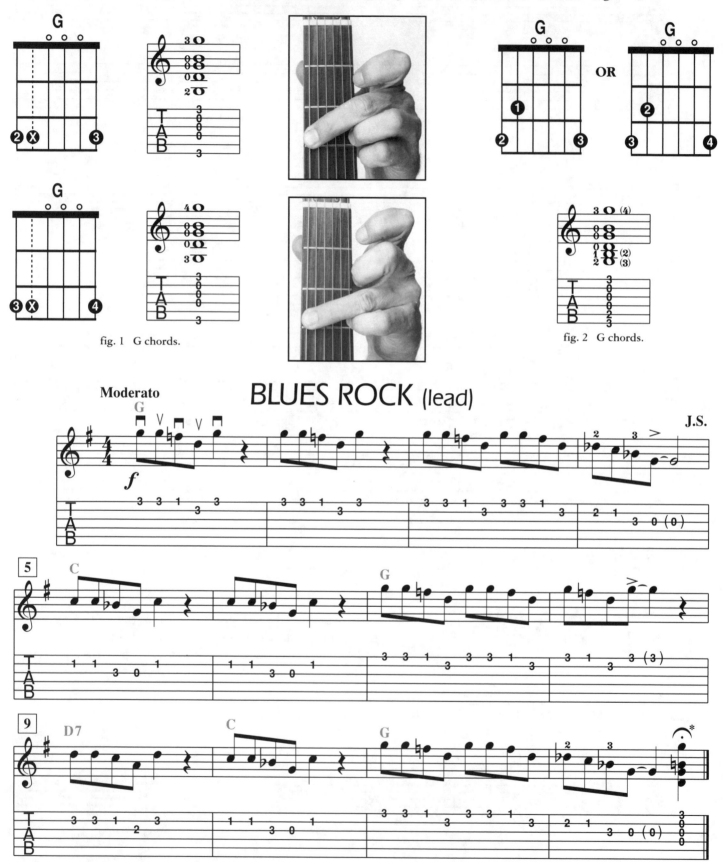

fig. 1 G chords.

fig. 2 G chords.

BLUES ROCK (lead)

*Fermata Sign (⌢). Also known as a hold, the fermata sign tells the player to sustain a note or chord, and to release it at his or her discretion.

BLUES ROCK (rhythm-accompaniment)

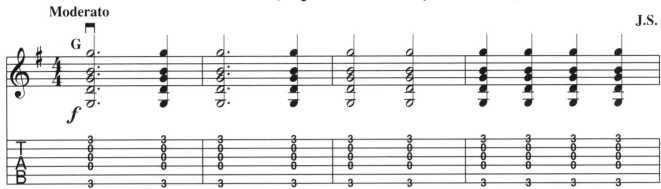

C Chord **full**

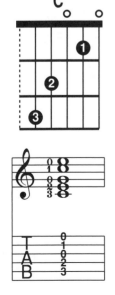

This is a full **C CHORD**. Avoid touching the open 3rd and 1st strings. Keep the fingers arched and the fingernails short.

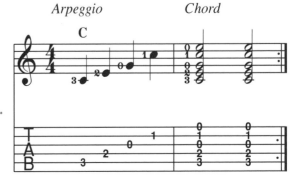

F Chord inside strings

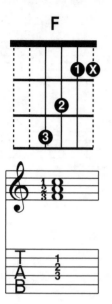

The **F CHORD** is played on the inside strings. Omit the 1st string from the chord. Dampen (❌) the 1st string with the side of the index finger.

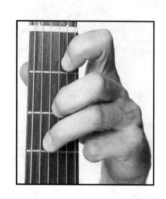

88.

Some chords have been added to create a solo chord arrangement of *Scarborough Fair*. Review the Dm chord on page 42 and the C chord on page 53.

SCARBOROUGH FAIR (solo)

Andante

Traditional

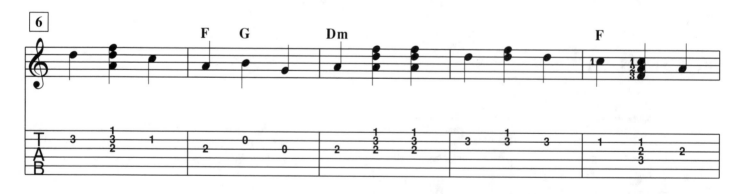

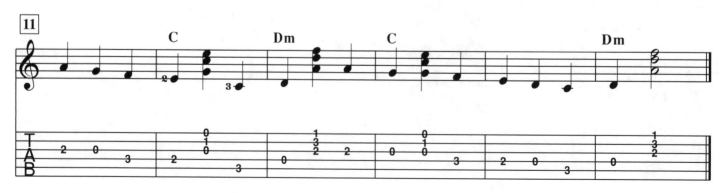

D Chord full

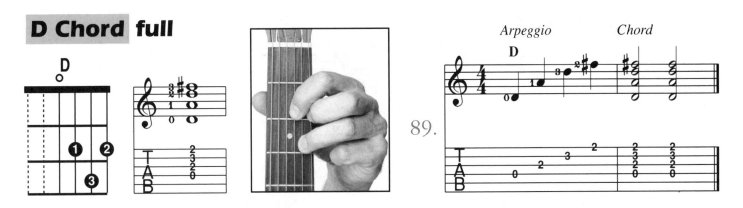

Arch the 3rd finger to avoid touching the 1st string when playing the **D CHORD**.

2/4 Time Signature

The 2/4 **TIME SIGNATURE** organizes the rhythm of the music into two beats per measure. The 1st beat of the measure should receive more emphasis or stress. Count: 1 2 1 2.

$\frac{2}{4}$ = Two beats in each measure
= A quarter note receives one beat

The melody for *House of the Rising Sun* is located in the bass line, which is embellished with occasional chords. Since the song moves at a moderate tempo, everything can be played with down-strokes.

HOUSE OF THE RISING SUN (solo)

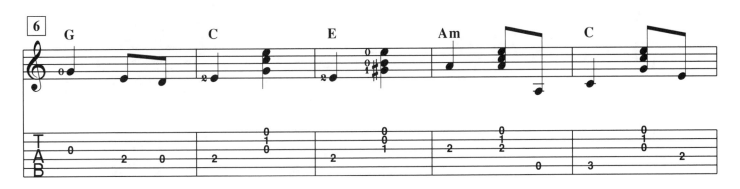

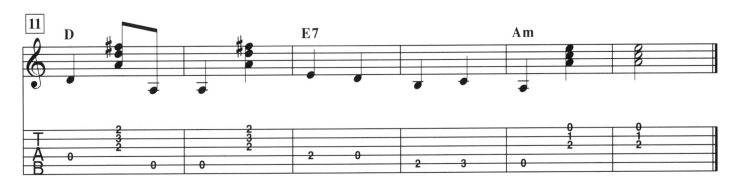

E⁶ and A⁶ Chords

The **E6** and **A6** are used in the accompaniment part of *Rhythm 'n' Blues*. These chords (fig. 1 and 2), are extensions of the *power chords* introduced on page 48.

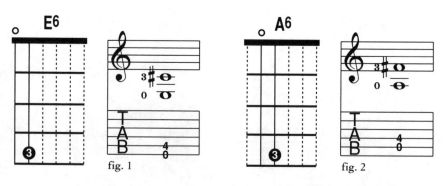

fig. 1   fig. 2

Practice exercises 90 and 91. Since you are going back and forth between the power chords (E5, A5) and the 6 chords (E6, A6), leave your index finger in place (in this case, on the 2nd fret).

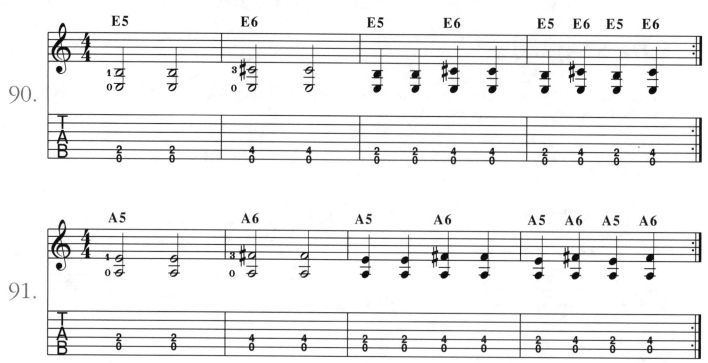

90.

91.

RHYTHM 'N' BLUES (accompaniment)

Moderato   J.S.

(continue pattern)

mf

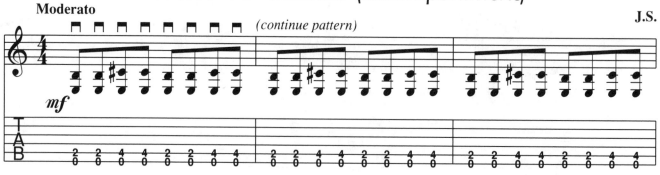

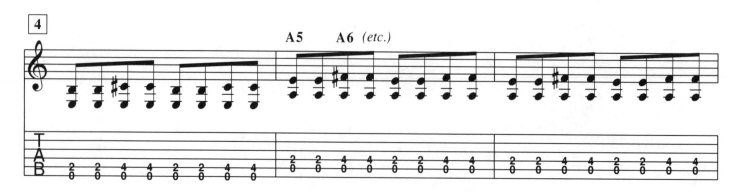

4

A5   A6 *(etc.)*

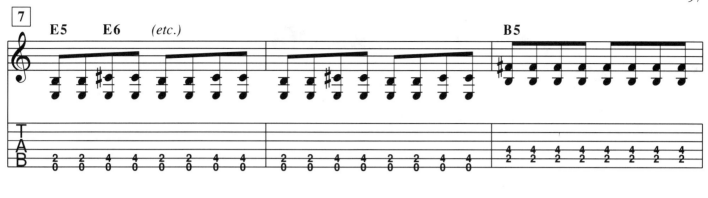

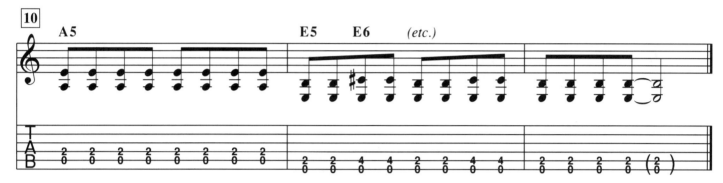

RHYTHM 'N' BLUES (lead)

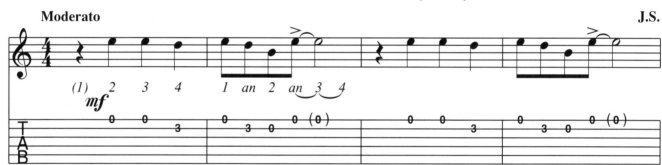

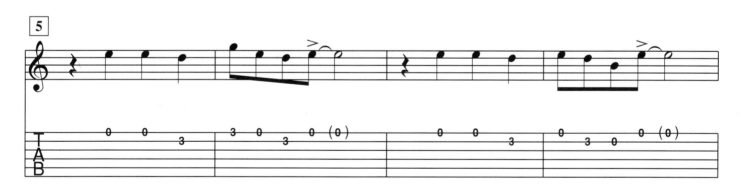

NOTE REVIEW

First Position

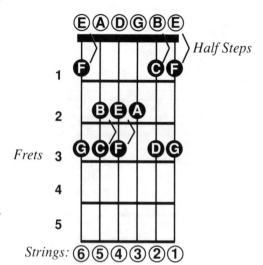

On the guitar, the name of the left-hand position is determined by the location of the index finger. In *1st position*, the index finger of the left hand is located at the 1st fret. Use the 1st finger to play the notes found on the 1st fret; that is, F on the 6th string, C on the 2nd string, and F on the 1st string. The 2nd finger should be used to play any note located on the 2nd fret. Use the 3rd finger for all notes located on the 3rd fret. Keep the fingers over the frets.

Play exercise 92 using down-strokes with a pick or alternating rest strokes with the index and middle fingers. Say the names of the notes as you play them. All of the notes are separated by a whole step with the exception of E to F and B to C, which are half steps. The *circled numbers* placed below various notes represent the guitar string.

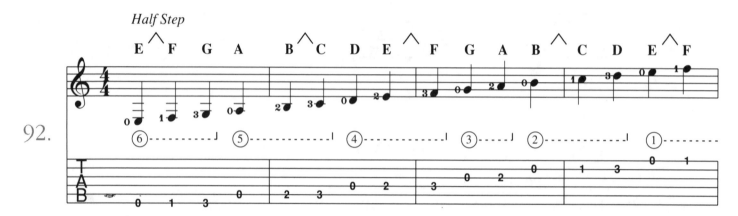

92.

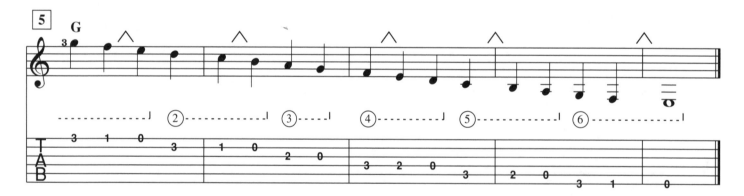

Sharps and Flats

A **SHARP** (♯) placed before a note in music notation *raises* the pitch of the note by one half step. On the guitar, that is the distance of one fret (fig. 1). A **FLAT** (♭) placed before a note in music notation *lowers* the pitch of the note by one half step (fig. 2).

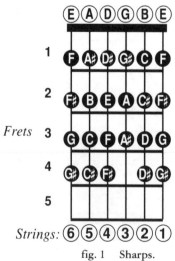

fig. 1   Sharps.

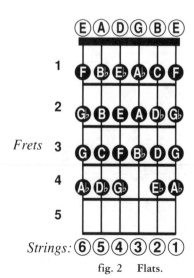

fig. 2   Flats.

Enharmonic Notes

The G♯ and A♭ in figures 1 and 2 are **ENHARMONIC** notes. They represent the *same* tone but they are *named* and *written* differently. Other examples of enharmonic notes are A♯ and B♭, C♯ and D♭, and F♯ and G♭.

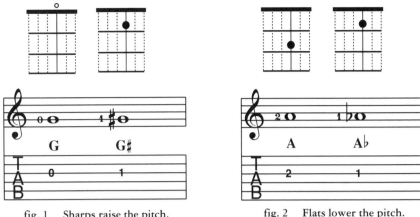

fig. 1   Sharps raise the pitch.   fig. 2   Flats lower the pitch.

Chromatic Scale

A **CHROMATIC SCALE** is a scale in which each successive note is a *half step* apart. The following exercise is a two-octave **E Chromatic Scale**. This scale begins on the open 6th string and moves upward to the open 1st string. In music notation, sharps are generally used on the ascending chromatic scale and flats are used on the descending chromatic scale.

KEY OF G (Review)

Key Signature

fig. 1

KEY has to do with the *tonal structure* of the music: **melody** (successive tones) and **harmony** (chords). A melody, song or exercise is in the **key of G Major** if it is based on the G major scale. The **KEY SIGNATURE** of a song is indicated at the beginning of each line of music. The key of G has one sharp (F#). All F's are played one half step higher (one fret higher in pitch) (fig. 1).

G Major Scale

The **MAJOR SCALE** is a series of eight successive tones that have a *specific pattern* of whole and half steps. There is always a half step between the 3rd and 4th tones and the 7th and 8th tones of the scale (fig. 2). The interval distance between the first note of the scale and the 8th note is called an **OCTAVE**. The following *G Scale Study* is a two-octave exercise. Notice the F# on the 4th and 1st strings. Use your 4th finger on the 4th string. It is important for the 4th finger to be comfortable and not to have to stretch and reach for the 4th fret. Favor the position of the 4th finger. It is shorter and cannot stretch and reach sideways as easily as the 1st finger.

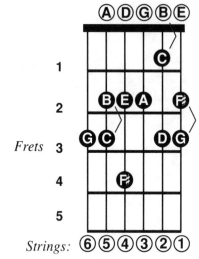

fig. 3 Two octave G scale.

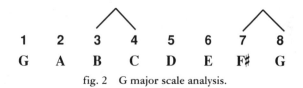

1	2	3	4	5	6	7	8
G	A	B	C	D	E	F#	G

fig. 2 G major scale analysis.

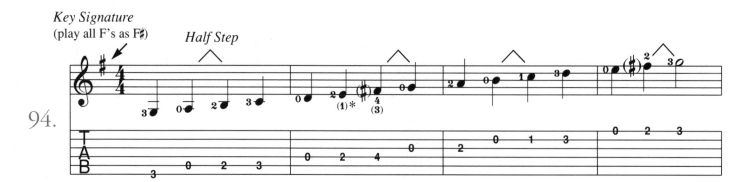

94.

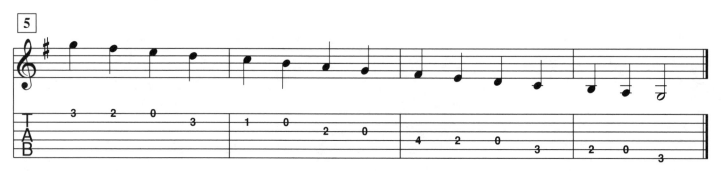

*Alternate fingering.

Second Position

Second Position was introduced on page 28. Shift the left hand up the fingerboard so that the index finger is on the 2nd fret. This is called the 2nd position because the 1st finger is located on the 2nd fret. Use the 4th finger to play the A, 5th fret, 1st string (fig. 4). Make certain that the knuckles of the 4th finger are bent.

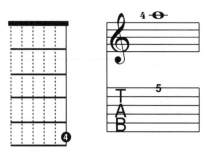

fig. 4 Second position A.

In exercise 95, **shift** to the *2nd position* in measure 4. Shift back to the 1st position in measure 5. At fast tempos or speeds, alternate the pick (⊓ ∨).

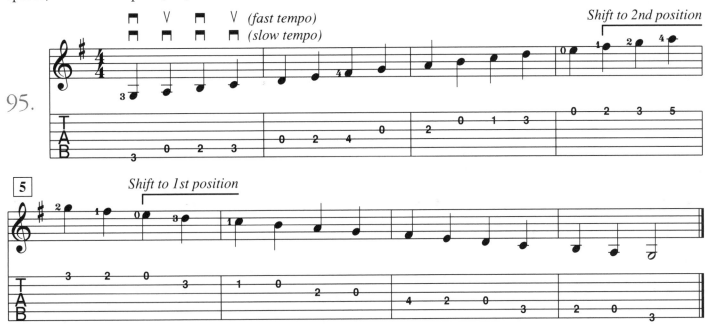

CHALLENGE Second Position G Scale

CHALLENGE sections will occur at various places in this book to present *optional* material. The **2nd Position G Scale** is a *moveable* two octave scale. Learn the scale by studying the chord frame diagrams of notes and fingerings (fig. 1 and 2). For future reference, the moveable G scale is written in standard music notation below. Try playing this scale pattern in other positions.

fig. 1   Fingering.

fig. 2   Notes.

Technique. Beginning with the G on the 6th string, play each note four times as you progress up and then down the scale. First play successive down-strokes and then play the scale using alternating down- and up-strokes. The left hand must be in a comfortable and balanced position to play the notes that occur on the 4th finger.

Principal Chords

Chords or harmonies used to accompany the melody or songs are also derived from the major scale. The **PRINCIPAL CHORDS** in the Key of G (see page 27) are chords constructed on the 1st (I), 4th (IV) and 5th (V) tones of the scale. In the Key of G, the principal chords are G, C and D7 (fig. 1).

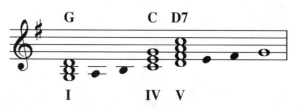

fig. 1   Principal chords in G.

The G chord functions as *home base* and is called the **Tonic**. The C chord (IV) is called the **Sub-dominant** and the D7 chord (V) is called the **Dominant**. Memorize the root (R) and 5th (5) for each chord. The root (R) is the *primary bass* note. The 5th (5) of the chord is the *alternate bass* note.

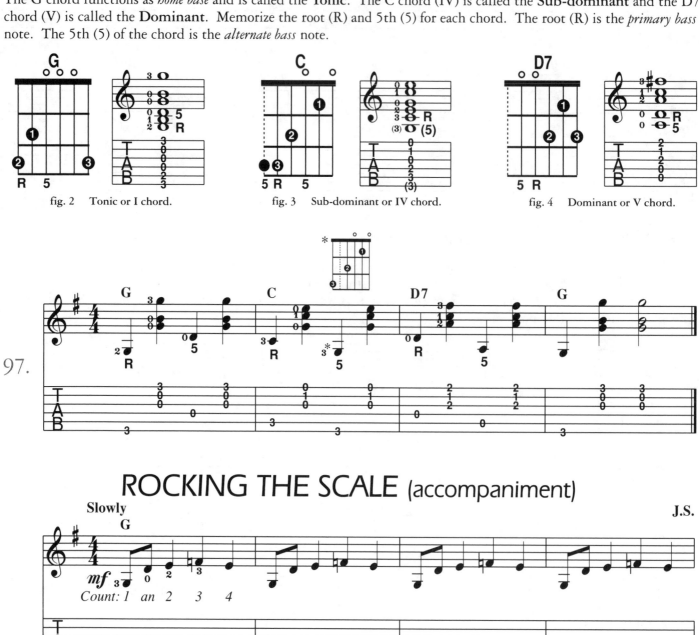

fig. 2   Tonic or I chord.   fig. 3   Sub-dominant or IV chord.   fig. 4   Dominant or V chord.

97.

ROCKING THE SCALE (accompaniment)

Slowly

J.S.

Count: 1 an 2   3   4

Exercise 98 is a preparatory drill for learning how to play the lead part to *Rocking the Scale*. Shift the hand to *2nd position* in measure 3. Use down-strokes with a pick.

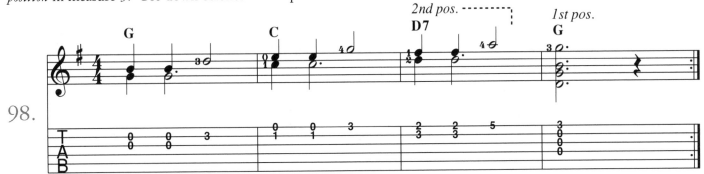

ROCKING THE SCALE (lead)

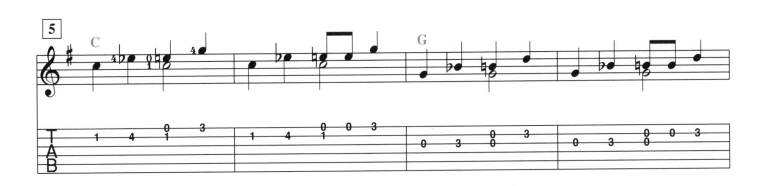

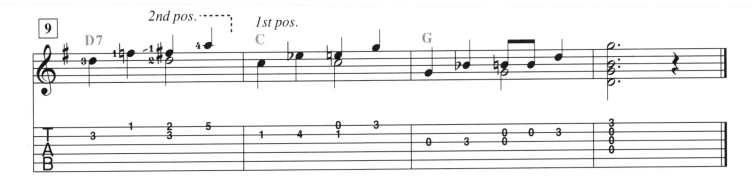

Moveable Power Chords

Power chords were introduced on page 48. Power chords only have two different notes in them (root and 5th). The root is usually doubled. These chords are typically used by *heavy metal* rock guitarists.

MOVEABLE POWER CHORDS can be played anywhere on the fingerboard of the guitar. Use the index finger to fret the lowest string as well as to dampen (❌) the treble strings (fig. 1, 2 and 3). The most effective playing technique is to use successive down-strokes with the pick as you *mute* the strings with the heel of your right hand. Play the accompaniment part to *Deliver*.

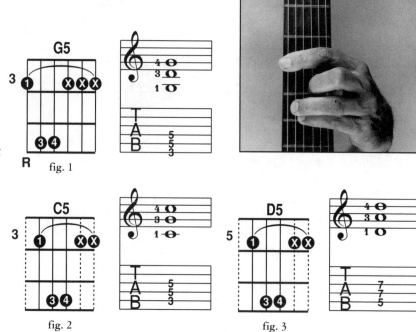

fig. 1

fig. 2

fig. 3

Rhythm Guitar:

DELIVER (accompaniment)

J.S.

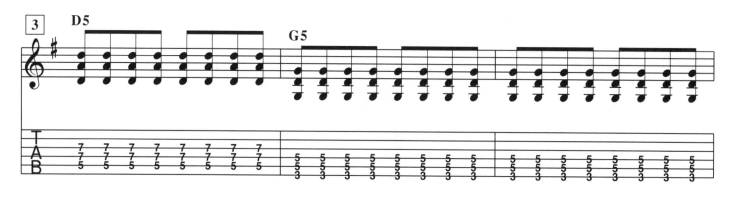

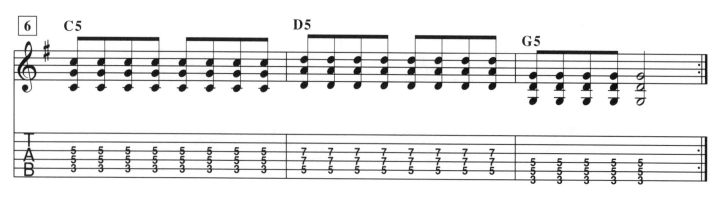

PENTATONIC MINOR SCALE

The **PENTATONIC MINOR SCALE** is a five-note scale that is widely used by rock guitarists (fig. 1). The structure of the scale makes it useful for improvisation (creating solos). This scale is also referred to as the **Rock Scale**. A third position, two-octave **G Pentatonic Minor Scale** is diagramed in figure 2 and is written in tablature in exercise 99.

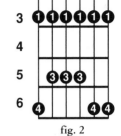

fig. 2

fig. 1   G Pentatonic Minor scale.

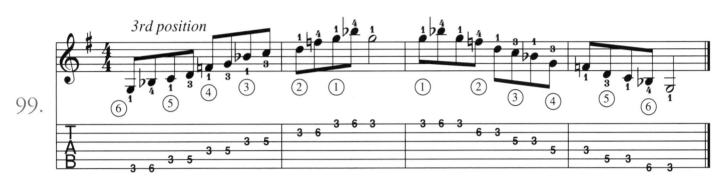

99.

Deliver is a *3rd position* **lead line solo** based on the G Pentatonic Minor Scale. Play straight eighths. For an additional **Challenge**, make up your own solo to these chord changes.

DELIVER (lead)

J.S.

Lively

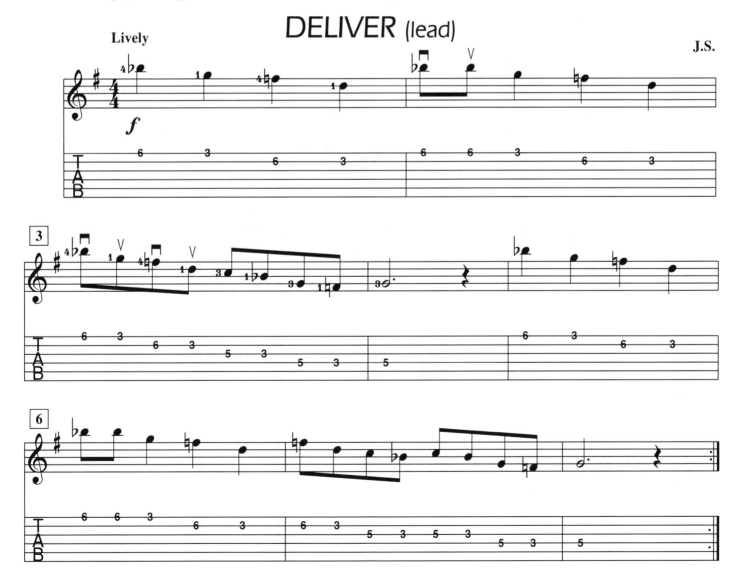

SECONDARY CHORDS
========================

In any major key, chords constructed on the 2nd (II), 3rd (III) and 6th (VI) degrees on the scale are called the **SECONDARY CHORDS**. In the Key of G Major, the **Secondary Chords** are Am (II), Bm (III) and Em (VI) (fig. 1). The II and VI chords are the most frequently used secondary chords.

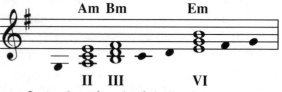

fig. 1   Secondary chords in G major.

Am Chord full

The root (R) of the **Am CHORD** is located on the open 5th string (A). The fifth (5) of the chord is located on the 4th string, 2nd fret (E). An alternate fifth is located on the open 6th string (E).

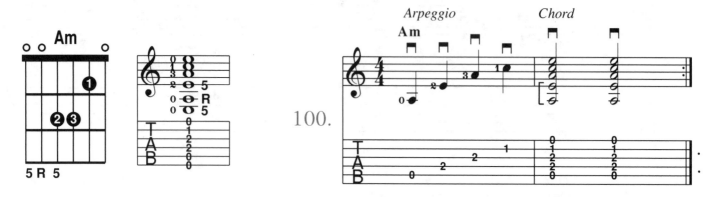

100.

II–V Chord Progression

Transportation Tip. A common chord progression in music is the II chord moving to the V chord. In the Key of G, this would be the Am to D7 progression. When moving back and forth between the Am and the D7 chord, leave the 1st finger on the 1st fret, 2nd string. This will help to guide the left hand. Practice the following exercise.

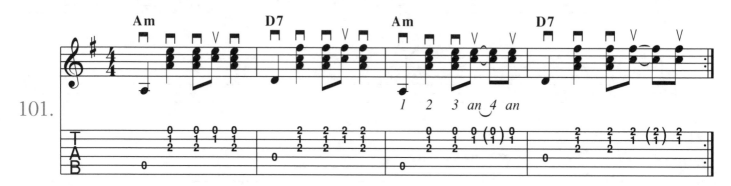

101.

Progress to Five is based on the II–V chord progression.

PROGRESS TO FIVE (accompaniment)

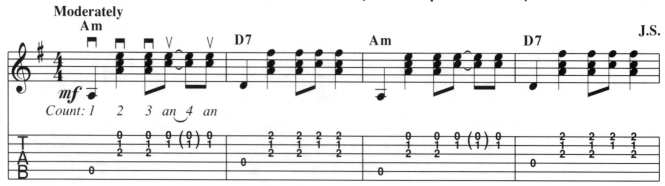

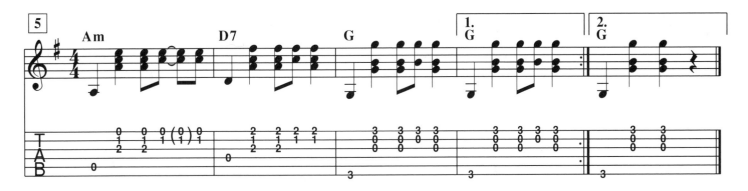

Dotted Quarter Note

When a **DOT** is added to a quarter note, it adds a half beat (½) to the value of the note. A **DOTTED QUARTER NOTE** receives one and one-half beats (1 + ½ = 1½).

The dotted quarter note is most often used in a **DOTTED QUARTER-EIGHTH NOTE** rhythm pattern. This pattern exists in the beginning of two familiar songs: *London Bridge* and *Deck the Halls*.

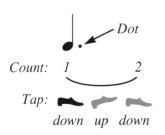

fig. 1 Dotted quarter note.

102.

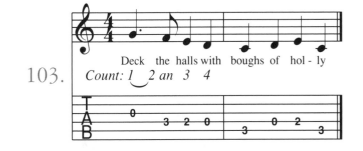

103.

PROGRESS TO FIVE (lead)

Moderately

J.S.

Em Chord full

The **Em CHORD** is the VI chord in the key of G major. The root (R) is located on the open 6th string (E) and on the 4th string, 2nd fret (E). The fifth (5) is located on the 5th string, 2nd fret (B).

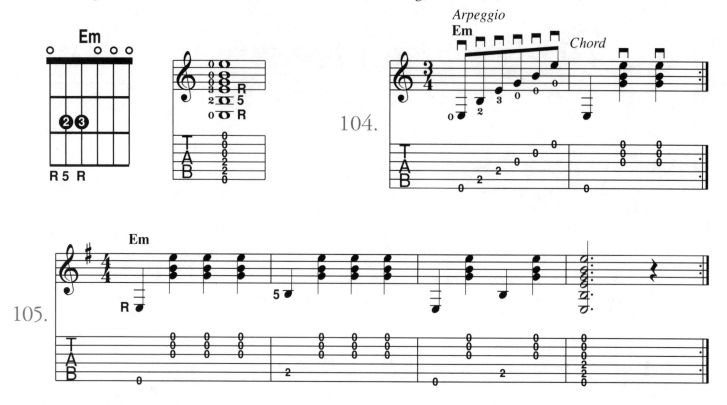

I–VI–II–V Chord Progression

A common chord progression, one that has given rise to many songs, is the **I–VI–II–V** progression. It works the same in every major key. Play the following exercises using either pickstyle or fingerstyle playing techniques. Memorize which tones are the **Root** (R) and **Fifth** (5) of each chord so you can alternate using them on the 1st and 3rd beats of the measure.

Transportation Tip. Practice going from the Em chord to the Am chord. Notice that the 2nd and 3rd fingers of the left hand are placed on the same fret in both of these chords. Lift these fingers together as you move from the 5th and 4th strings to the 4th and 3rd strings.

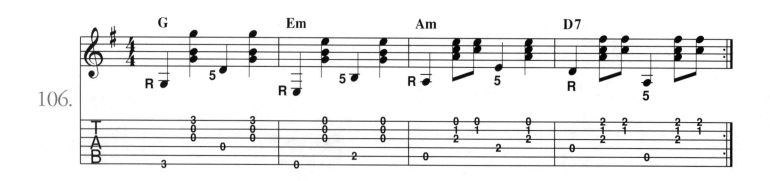

Sunday is a melody in the key of G that is based on the I–VI–II–V chord progression. After you learn the melody, record it and try playing a variety of accompaniment patterns with it.

SUNDAY (lead)

J.S.

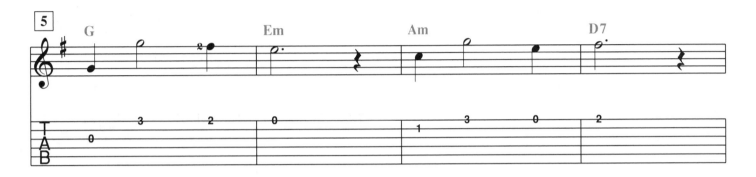

Bm7 Chord simplified

The III chord in the key of G is **Bm7**. The 4th string is omitted in this simplified version. Allow the index finger to lightly touch and deaden (prevent from vibrating) the 4th string. The root (R) is located on the 5th string, 2nd fret (B).

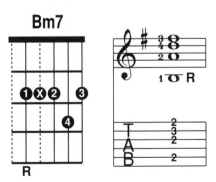

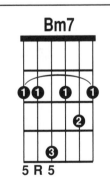

CHALLENGE Moveable Bm7 Chord

Place the index finger across all of the strings at the 2nd fret. Be as close to the fret wire as possible. The finger needs to be straight. Apply pressure on the side of the index finger (guitar nut side). Arch the wrist out. Place the thumb opposite the index finger.

Pinch Technique pickstyle

In pickstyle, the **PINCH TECHNIQUE** is done with the pick and middle finger plucking the strings simultaneously. Use the pick on the lower string and pluck the higher string with the middle finger.

107.

70

Measures 7, 8 and 10 of the accompaniment for *New Horizons* require the **pinch technique**. Review exercise 107 on page 69.

NEW HORIZONS (accompaniment)

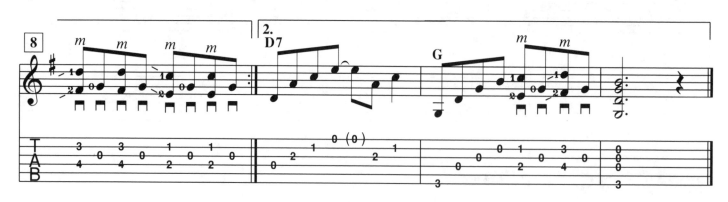

NEW HORIZONS (solo)

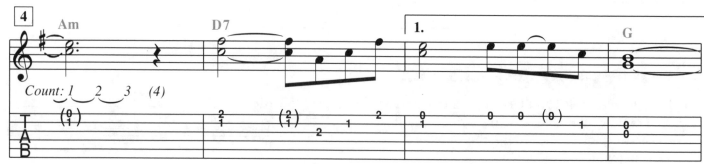

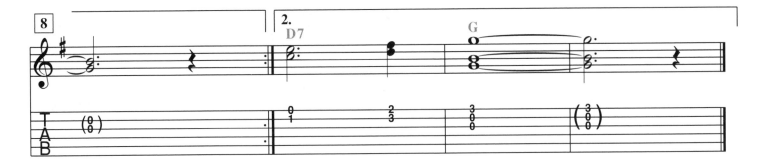

Extensions

When a fourth note is added to a basic triad (three note chord), the chord is said to be **EXTENDED**. For example, the D7 chord is an extended D Chord. All major and minor chords can be **extended**. A fourth note can be added to provide additional interest and color to the sound of these chords. In the key of G, the G chord (I) can be extended to a **G major 7th chord**. The C Chord (IV) can be extended to a **C major 7th chord** (fig. 1).

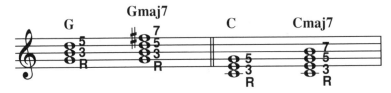

fig.1   Theory analysis.

Gmaj7 Chord

The root (R) of the **G major 7th chord** is located on the 6th string, 3rd fret (G). The fifth (5) of the chord is on the open 4th string (D). Dampen (✪ = prevent from sounding) the open 5th string by lightly touching it with the 2nd finger. Compared to the G7 chord (G dominant 7th) which is a chord that contains harmonic tension and demands resolution (usually to the C chord), the G maj7 chord is a relaxed "color" chord. It is an extension of the I chord (G) in the key of G.

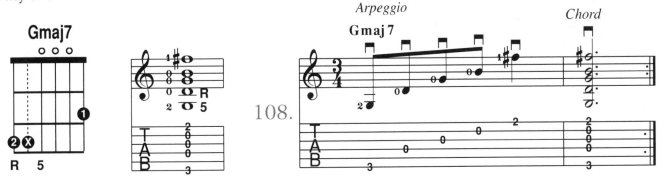

108.

Cmaj7 Chord

The root (R) of the **C major 7th chord** is located on the 5th string, 3rd fret (C). To play the fifth (5) of the chord (G), move the 3rd finger to the 6th string, 3rd fret (G). The Cmaj7 chord is an extended IV chord in the key of G.

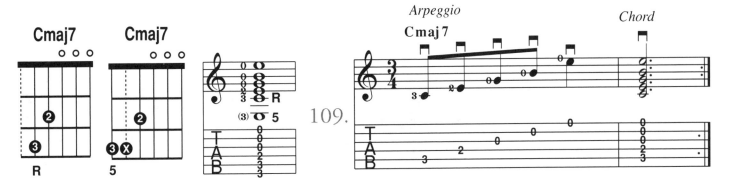

109.

BLUES IN G

Triplets

Count: 1   an   ah

Say: Trip - a - let

Tap:

A **TRIPLET** is a rhythm pattern that divides the basic quarter note beat into three equal parts. It is a group of three eighth notes that are played in the space of one count or beat.

Tap the rhythm of exercise 110 on your guitar. Tap your foot on the downbeats and count: *1 2 3 4.*

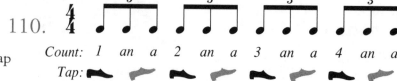

110.

Count: 1   an   a   2   an   a   3   an   a   4   an   a

Tap:

Use a down-up-down (⊓ V ⊓) or an up-down-up (V ⊓ V) pattern when playing triplets. Play exercise 111. **SIMILE** is a term used in music that means "to continue playing in a *similar* manner."

111.

Shuffle Rhythm

A major characteristic of the "blues" is the **SHUFFLE RHYTHM**. This basic beat is derived from sub-dividing the beat into three parts (fig. 1). The downbeat combines the time value of the 1st two notes of the triplet and the upbeat receives the value of the third note (fig. 2).

Count: 1   an   a

Say: trip - a - let

fig. 1

Count: 1 — an   a

Say: trip - a - let   trip - let

fig. 2

Since rhythm patterns are often repeated several times, an abbreviated *slash* notation is often used to notate rhythm guitar parts (fig. 4).

Count: 1   2   an   3   4   an

fig. 3   Pickstyle.

Count: 1   2   an   3   4   an

fig. 4   Slash notation.

Exercise 112 is the **shuffle rhythm** on the G chord. Accent (>) the 1st and 3rd downbeats of this rhythm pattern.

112.

Count: 1   a   2   a   3   a   4   a

12-Bar Blues

Chord exercise 113 is a basic **12-BAR BLUES** progression in the key of G. Play the shuffle rhythm on each chord. The **REPEAT SIGN** (⁄.) used in measures 2–12 is an abbreviation that is used in music notation. It means to repeat the rhythm notated in the previous measure.

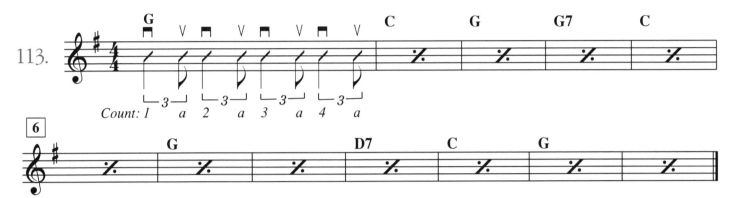

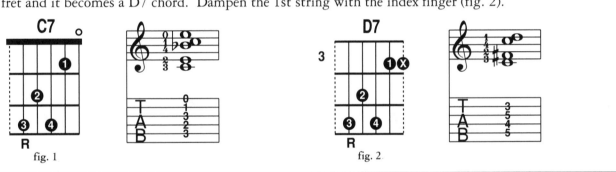

CHALLENGE Moveable Dominant 7th Chord, 5th String Root

The following moveable dominant 7th chord form can substitute for the C and D7 chords in the 12-Bar Blues, exercise 113. The C7 chord (fig. 1) will replace the C chord. Move this dominant 7th chord form to the 3rd fret and it becomes a D7 chord. Dampen the 1st string with the index finger (fig. 2).

fig. 1

fig. 2

Swing Eighths

In the Blues and Jazz styles of performance, the basic beat is subdivided into three parts (triplets). The blues shuffle rhythm was described on page 72. The traditional music notation system required to write these triplet rhythm figures would be very cumbersome. Fortunately, there is a performance practice among blues and jazz musicians to *play* **SWING EIGHTHS** when they see *written* **STRAIGHT EIGHTHS** (fig. 3). Swing eighths (also called jazz eighths) are played as if there were a group of three notes (triplets) with the first note tied to the middle note (fig. 4).

Straight Eighths = *Swing Eighths* or *Straight Eighths* = *Swing Eighths*

Written / *Played* — fig. 3   *Written* / *Played* — fig. 4

This performance practice makes it unnecessary for publishers to have to write blues and jazz songs in triplets. It is sufficient to indicate at the beginning of the music if the eighths are to be performed as **swing eighths**. Exercise 114 is the written example, and exercise 115 shows in traditional notation how exercise 114 should sound when played.

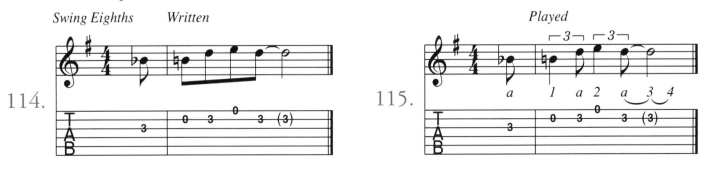

Hesitation is a solo based on the 12-bar blues progression. The solo moves temporarily into the 3rd position on the last upbeat of measures 1 and 4. In the 3rd position, the index finger is located on the 3rd fret. The melody then moves back into 1st position. Isolate and practice these measures. Exercise 113 on page 73 can be used as an accompaniment to this song. All of the eighths in this solo need to be interpreted as **swing eighths**.

HESITATION (lead)

The following accompaniment to *Hesitation* requires the use of the pinch technique pickstyle which was introduced on page 69. Practice exercise 116 for a review of the pinch technique. Use the pick on the low notes and the middle finger to play the higher notes.

116.

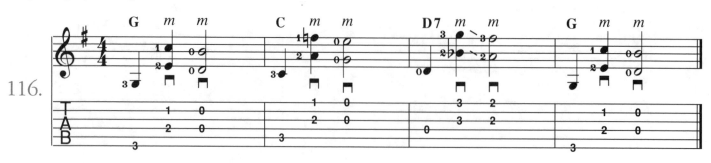

Exercises 117 and 118 are a review of how to play swing eighths. Exercise 117 is the *written* example and exercise 118 is how exercise 117 should sound and be played.

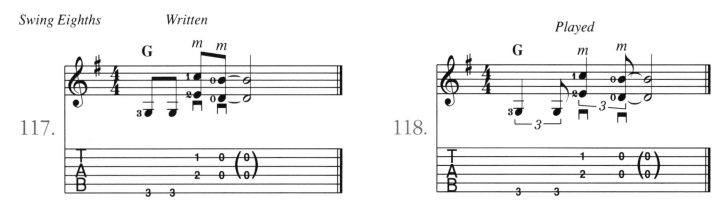

Now play the accompaniment for *Hesitation*. To help you keep a steady beat, count the tied notes. There is a tendency to rush ahead on tied notes.

HESITATION (accompaniment)

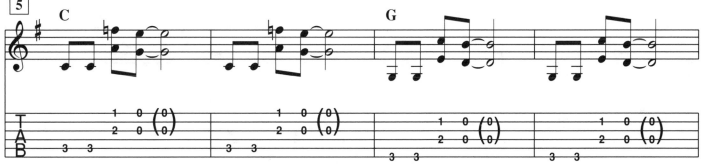

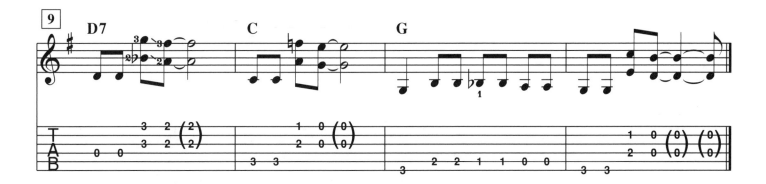

*From this point on, if a blues or jazz style is desired, **swing eighths** will be indicated at the beginning of the music.

MINOR BLUES

Blues for Bobbie (lead) is based on a jazz variation of the **MINOR BLUES** chord progression. This chord progression contains a new chord—F♯m7♭5 (F sharp minor 7th flat five) which will be explained on page 77. The eighths in this solo need to be interpreted as **swing eighths** (see page 73).

Syncopation

Blues for Bobbie contains many examples of **syncopation** (see page 45). In 4/4 time, the normal accent (>) is on the 1st beat of the measure with a secondary accent on the 3rd beat. In general, downbeats receive more emphasis than upbeats. When this accent is shifted to a weak beat (such as an upbeat—*an*), it is called syncopation. Measure 1 contains two examples of syncopation. Both the E and the B are played on an upbeat, and are the longest notes in the measure. They need to be stressed. In measure 3, the syncopated note is the low E.

Alternate the pick. Use down-strokes (⊓) on the downbeats and up-strokes (V) on the upbeats. Play the accents (>) louder.

Swing Eighths

BLUES FOR BOBBIE (lead)

J.S.

F#m7♭5 Chord

The **F#m7♭5 CHORD** (F sharp minor seventh flat five) is the first **altered** chord presented in this book. The flatted fifth (♭5) is one 1/2 step lower than the fifth in a normal minor triad. This chord is sometimes written as F#m7-5. The dash (-) indicates to flat the fifth. Dampen the 5th string with the 2nd finger (fig. 1).

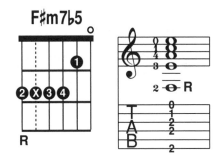

Play the accompaniment for *Blues for Bobbie*. Remember to swing the eighths.

BLUES FOR BOBBIE (accompaniment)

Jazz 12-bar blues

The basic 12-bar blues progression was introduced on page 73. The jazz version of the blues generally includes more chord changes and the chords are usually extended and altered (more on this later). In *Jazz Blues*, the Am (II chord) is extended to an Am7 (fig. 1) and the C (IV chord) is extended to a C7 (fig. 2).

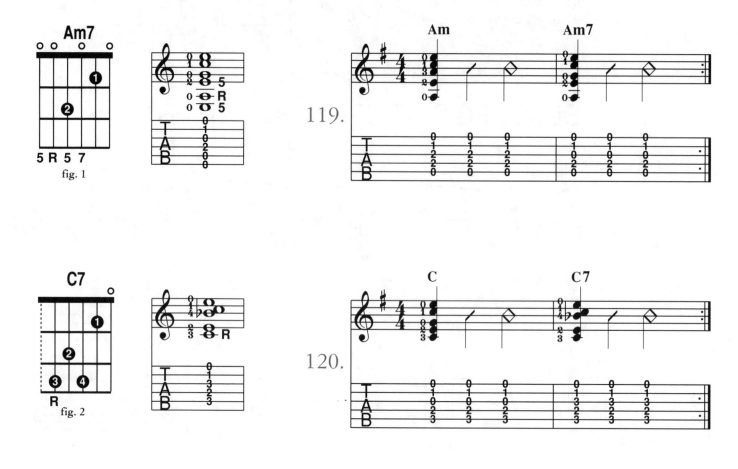

fig. 1

fig. 2

119.

120.

Transportation Tip. The best fingering to use for the G chord when moving to the C7 is diagramed in figure 3. Practice exercise 121.

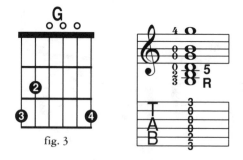

fig. 3

Swing Eighths

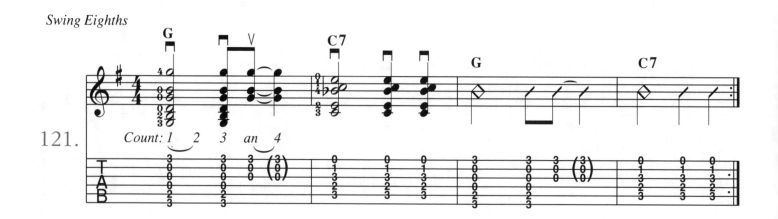

121.

Count: *1 2 3 an 4*

Review the E7 chord (page 51) and the Bm7 chord (page 69).
The chord diagrams are included here for reference (fig. 1).

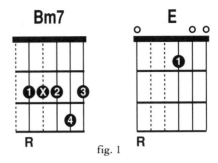

Before playing the entire accompaniment for *Jazz Blues*, practice measures 11 and 12 to review the Gmaj7 chord (see page 71). These two measures are called the "turn around" in jazz. They take you back to the beginning of the song. Remember to swing the eighths.

Swing Eighths

JAZZ BLUES (accompaniment)

JAZZ BLUES (solo)

The accented notes (>) in the *Jazz Blues* solo need to be emphasized. Move into 2nd position at measure 8 and back into 1st position at measure 9. Once again, interpret all eighth note patterns as swing eighths.

KEY OF C

C Major Scale

The **C MAJOR SCALE** is constructed exactly like the G major scale (see page 60). There are half steps between the 3rd and 4th tones and the 7th and 8th tones of the scale (fig. 1).

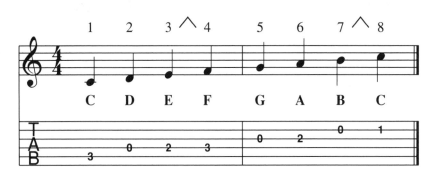

fig. 1   C major scale.

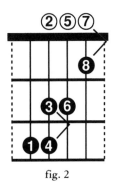 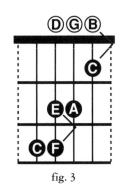

fig. 2   fig. 3

The fretboard analysis to the left will help you to visualize the **C Major Scale**. Figure 2 is an analysis by whole step and half step. Figure 3 is a fretboard analysis by note names.

Practice the following *C Scale Study* using successive down-strokes (⊓) at a slow to moderate speed. Alternate the pick (⊓ V) at faster speeds. I recommend that you get a metronome to help develop speed and a good sense of time.

C SCALE STUDY

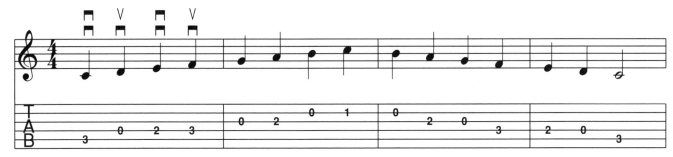

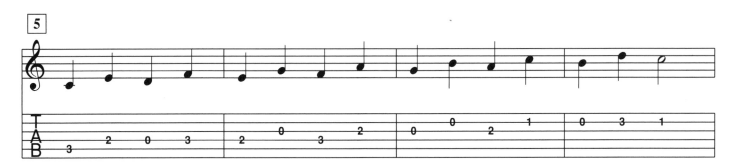

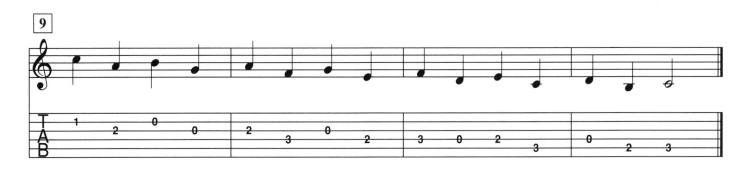

CHALLENGE Second Position C Scale

The Second Position C Scale is a *moveable* scale. Learn the scale by studying the chord frame diagrams of the fingerings and notes (fig. 1 and 2).

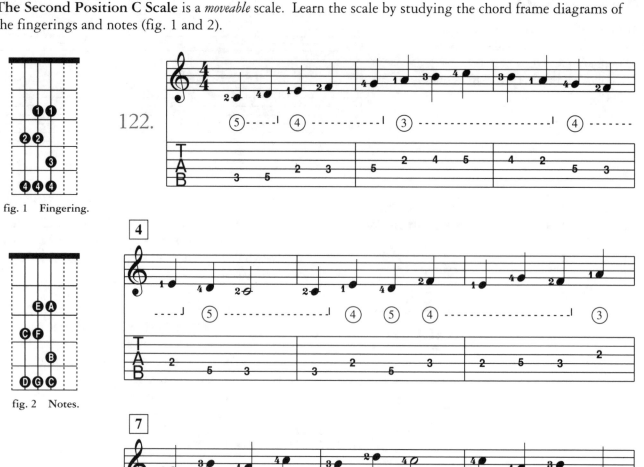

fig. 1 Fingering.

fig. 2 Notes.

Principal Chords

As mentioned on page 62, the **PRINCIPAL CHORDS** in a major key are the chords constructed on the 1st (I), 4th (IV) and 5th (V) tones of the scale. They are called the **tonic** (I), **sub-dominant** (IV) and **dominant** (V) chords. In the Key of C, the principal chords are C, F and G7 (fig. 3).

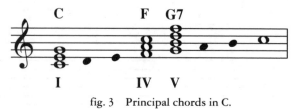

fig. 3 Principal chords in C.

C Chord extensions

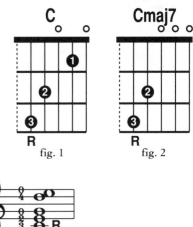

C   Cmaj7

fig. 1   fig. 2

The C chord (page 62) and the Cmaj7 chord (page 71) were presented in the key of G where they function as IV chords. In the Key of C, they function as I chords (fig. 1 and 2). To add additional interest, tension and variety to the color of the C chord, a 9th (an octave above the 2nd) can be added above the root of the chord. The 9th and the 2nd are the same note (D). In today's popular music, this chord is either called a Cadd9 or a Cadd2 chord (fig. 3).

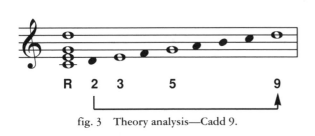

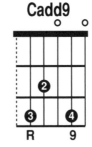 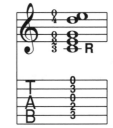

R   2   3   5   9

fig. 3   Theory analysis—Cadd 9.

Cadd9

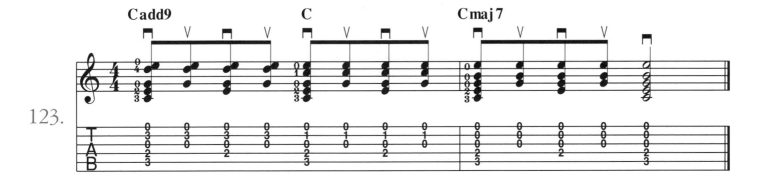

123.

G7 Chord full

After the C chord, the **G7 CHORD** is the most frequently used chord in the key of C. The root (R) of the chord is located on the 6th string, 3rd fret (G). The fifth (5) is located on the open 4th string (D).

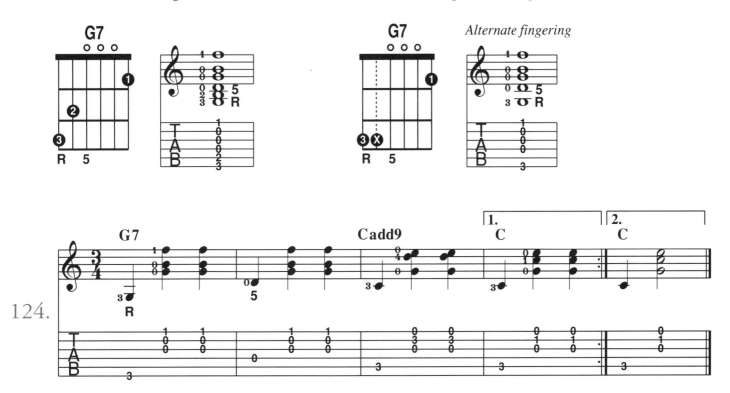

124.

84

F Chord small bar

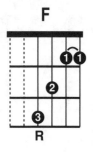 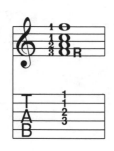 

The *small bar* **F CHORD** requires the 1st finger of the left hand to cover (fret) two strings—the 1st and 2nd strings. The pressure needs to be on the side of the index finger. Build the chord from the 4th string (fig. 1). Once you have placed the index finger on the 2nd string, roll the index finger toward the nut of the guitar as you cover the 1st string (fig. 2). Since the strings are lower and the frets are narrower at the 5th fret of the guitar, practice the small bar chord in 5th position. Remember: the name of a position on the guitar is determined by the location of the left hand index finger. If your index finger is on the 5th fret, you are in 5th position (fig. 3).

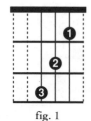 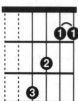 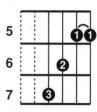

fig. 1
Build the F chord from the 4th string

fig. 2
Roll the index finger on to the 1st string

fig. 3
Practice the small bar in 5th position

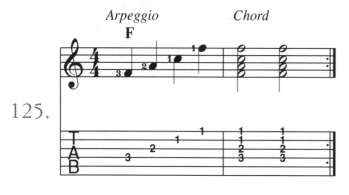 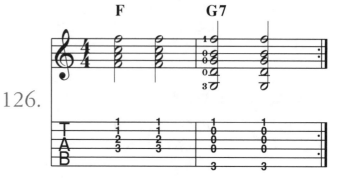

125.

126.

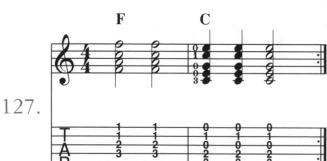 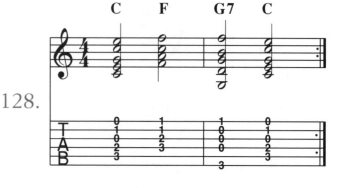

127.

128.

Alternate bass

The fifth (5) for the small bar F chord is located on the 5th string, 3rd fret (C). Two methods can be used to play the fifth. Move the 3rd finger back and forth between the 4th and 5th strings (fig. 4), or use the five string version of the small bar F chord (fig. 5).

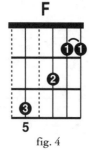 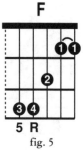

fig. 4

fig. 5

129.

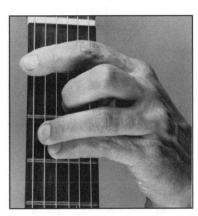

CHALLENGE Full Bar F and G7 Chords - 6th String Root

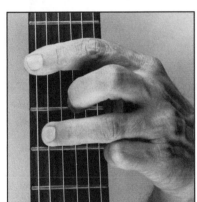

fig. 1   Full bar G7 chord.

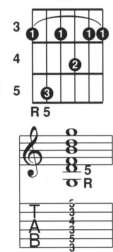

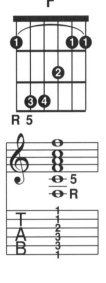

fig. 2   Full bar F chord.

The **Full Bar F** and **G7** chords require you to cover (fret) all six strings with the index finger. To develop the ability to play the full bar, I recommend that you 1st apply it at the 5th fret. At the 5th fret, the strings are closer to the fingerboard and the frets are closer together. This makes it easier to form the bar chords.

The index finger must be straight. Slightly arch the wrist out (away from the neck) and place the thumb opposite the index finger in a grip position. The palm of the hand should not touch the neck of the guitar (fig. 3).

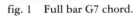

fig. 3

Now add the 2nd and 3rd fingers to play the **dominant 7th form** of the 6th string root bar chord (fig. 4). Once you can play this chord at the 5th fret, move it down (down in pitch) to the 3rd fret to play the **G7 chord** (fig. 1).

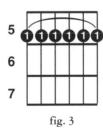

fig. 4
Dominant
7th chord.

To play the **Full Bar F chord**, add the 4th finger to the 4th string, 3rd fret (fig. 2). Initially, try forming this major chord at the 5th fret (fig. 5). Once you can play it at the 5th fret, move it to the 1st fret to play the F chord.

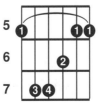

fig. 5   Major chord.

Secondary Chords

Chords constructed on the II, III and VI degrees of the major scale are called **SECONDARY CHORDS**. In the key of C, the **Secondary Chords** are **Dm** (II), **Em** (III) and **Am** (VI) (fig. 1).

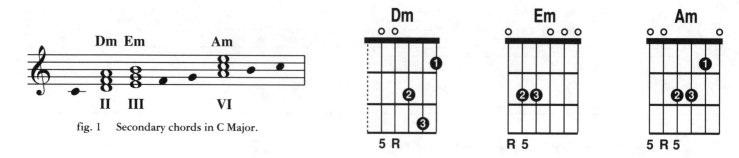

fig. 1   Secondary chords in C Major.

Exercise 130 drills the **Principal** and **Secondary Chords** in the key of C.

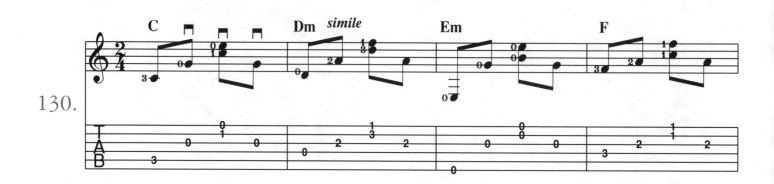

130.

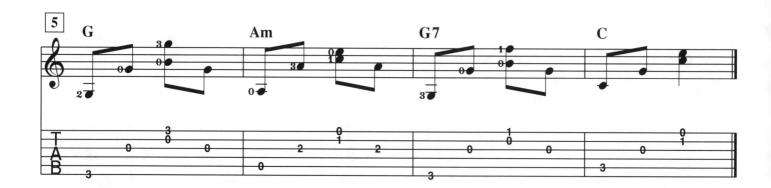

FRESH AIR (accompaniment)

FRESH AIR (lead)

J.S.

Fmaj7 Chord

The **Fmaj7 Chord** is an extended F chord (IV chord) in the key of C. The 7th (E) is added to the chord. The root (R) of the chord is located on the 4th string, 3rd fret (F).

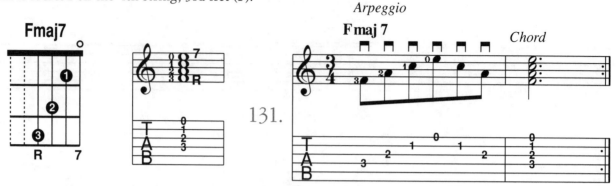

131.

In preparation for playing the accompaniment to *Soft Rock*, practice exercise 132. The natural gravitation of the II chord (Dm) is to the V chord (G7).

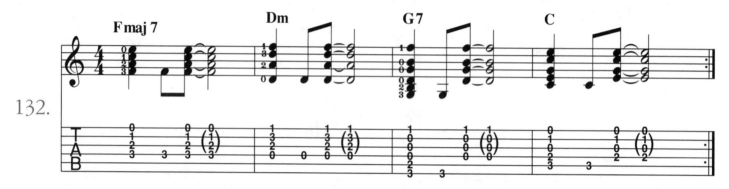

132.

For clarification on how to play measures 1, 2, 7 and 8, review the Cadd9–C–Cmaj7 chord progression introduced on page 83. *Soft Rock* is typical of some of the soft rock ballads that are popular today.

SOFT ROCK (accompaniment)

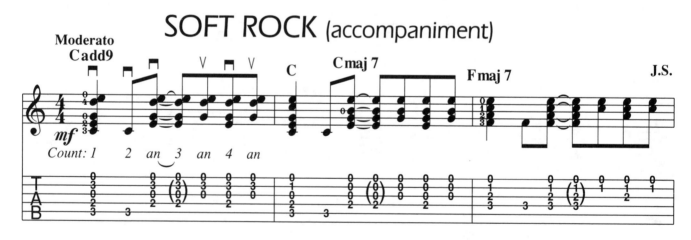

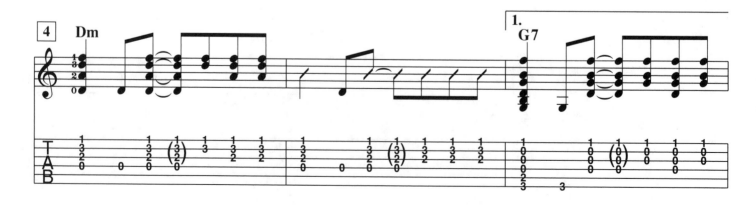

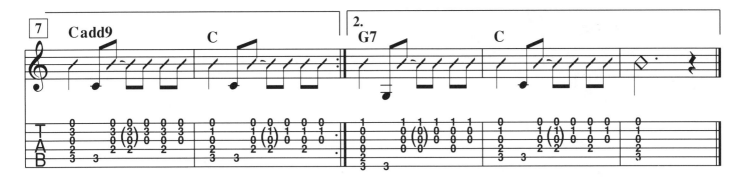

Sixteenth Notes

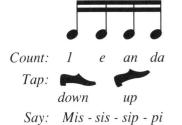

fig. 1 Sixteenth notes.

A **SIXTEENTH NOTE** receives one-fourth of a count or beat. Four sixteenth notes equal one beat (fig. 1).

Two sixteenth notes are equal in time value to one eighth note (fig. 2). Four sixteenth notes have the combined time value of one quarter note (fig. 3).

fig. 2

fig. 3

SOFT ROCK (lead)

J.S.

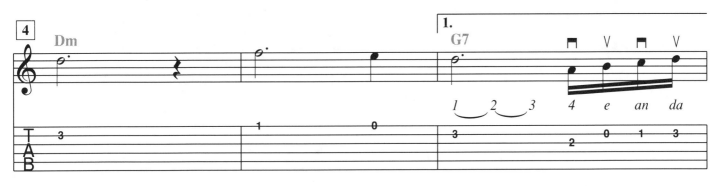

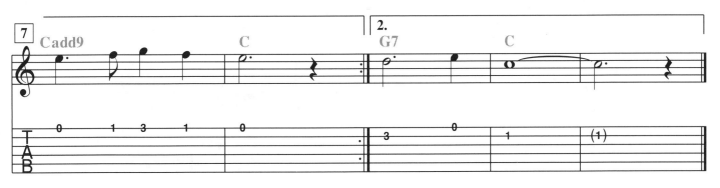

90

Dm7 and Dm#7 Chords

In the Key of C, the secondary chords Dm (II), Em (III) and Am (VI) can all be extended to minor 7th chords. You have already been introduced to the Am7 chord (see page 78). The Dm7 chord adds a 7th (C) above the root (fig. 1). The Dm#7 chord is an **altered chord**. The 7th (C) is sharped, or raised a 1/2 step (C#) (fig. 2).

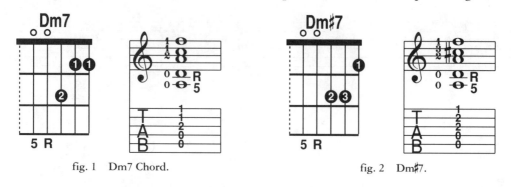

fig. 1   Dm7 Chord.   fig. 2   Dm#7.

LAMENT (accompaniment)

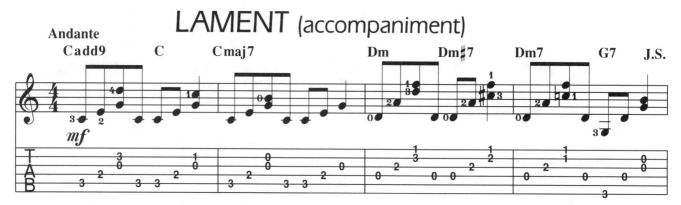

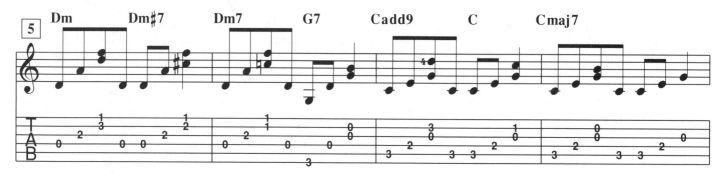

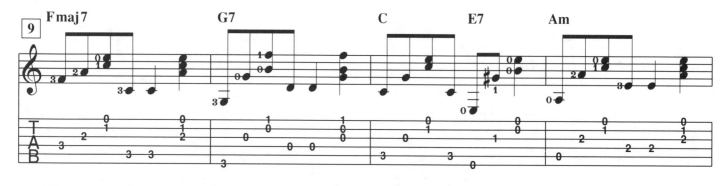

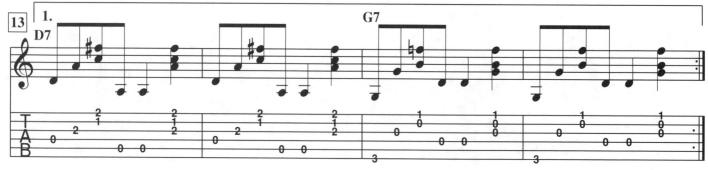

LAMENT (lead)

BLUES IN A

Principal Chords

In the key of A, the **PRINCIPAL CHORDS** are A, D and E7. When playing the blues, the D chord (IV) is often extended to a D7 (dominant 7th) chord. The **shuffle rhythm** is a major characteristic of the blues (see page 72) so the eighth notes are played as **swing eighths** (see page 73). Learn to play the **A CHORD** (fig. 1) and review the D7 and E7 chords (fig. 2 and 3) as preparation for playing exercise 133.

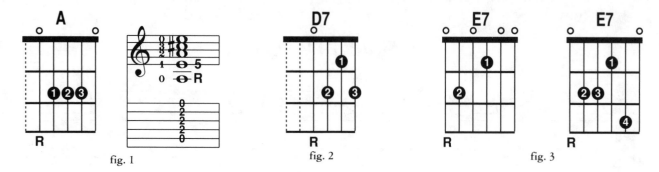

fig. 1   fig. 2   fig. 3

8-Bar Blues

The **8-BAR BLUES** is a variation of the 12-Bar Blues introduced on page 72. Practice the chord changes. **Transportation Tip:** the easiest way to play the A7 chord when it follows an A chord is to lift the 2nd finger (fig. 4).

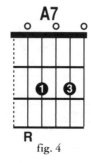

fig. 4

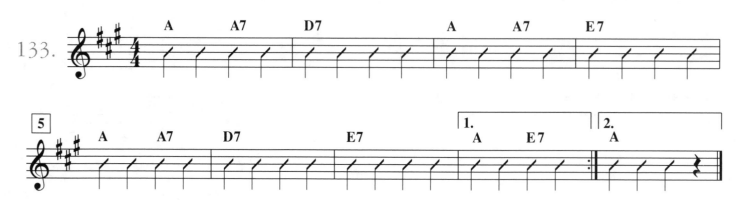

Rhythm Guitar

Exercise 134 is a blues shuffle-rhythm pattern that can be played on each chord and in each measure of the 8-Bar Blues (exercise 133). The written eighth notes are to be played as swing eighths. In pickstyle, use alternating down and up strokes.

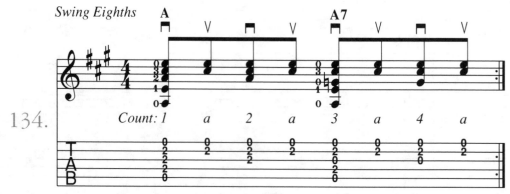

Mute Technique. Exercise 136 is the same exercise as 134 with one exception—the 2nd and 4th beats of the measure are **muted**. Muting is a right-hand technique that dampens (silences) the strings immediately following a downward strum or scratch. Strum or scratch down across the strings (bass to treble) and then immediately **mute** the strings by rolling onto the strings with the side or heel of the right hand. This should be done as one continuous motion. The *primary* motion is in the wrist as you open the hand and roll on to its side. As a preparatory drill, play exercise 135 on open strings. Practice the rhythm pattern in exercise 136 using the A, A7, D7 and E7 chords and then play the 8-Bar Blues on page 92.

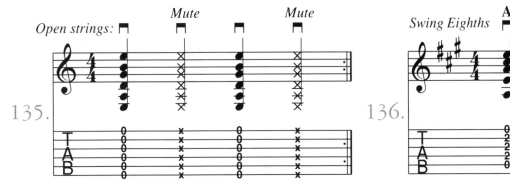

135.

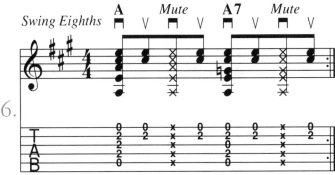

136.

CHALLENGE Moveable Chords

Major & Dominant 7th Chords 6th String Root

On page 85, techniques for playing and developing a **FULL BAR** Major and **Dominant 7th** chord were introduced. When these chord forms are moved to the 5th fret, they become an **A chord** (fig. 1) and an **A7 chord** (fig. 2).

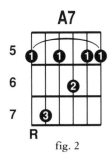

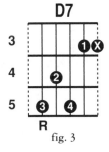

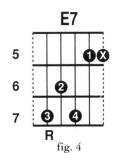

Dominant 7th Chords 5th String Root

On page 73, a moveable **D7 chord** was introduced (fig. 3). When moved to the 5th fret, this chord becomes an **E7 chord** (fig. 4).

Damp Technique. With moveable chords, a damp technique is used to stop the strings from vibrating instead of a mute. In exercise 137, release the pressure but maintain contact on the strings on beats 2 and 4.

Play the 8-Bar Blues (page 92) using the *moveable* A, D7 and E7 chords.

137.

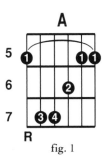

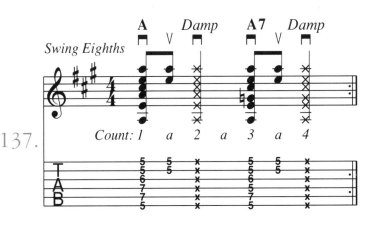

BLUES SCALE

fig. 1 A blues scale.

The **BLUES SCALE** is a six-note scale that is widely used by blues and jazz guitarists (fig. 1). It is very similar to the Pentatonic Minor Scale introduced on page 65. However, the **Blues Scale** includes a flatted 5th. A 5th position, two octave **A Blues Scale** is diagramed in (fig. 2) and is written in tablature in exercise 138. *Easy Does It* is a **lead line solo** based on the A Blues Scale. It can be accompanied with either open or moveable chords.

fig. 2

EASY DOES IT (lead)

J.S.

Swing Eighths   Slow

CHALLENGE Make up your own solo based on the chord changes and the A Blues Scale used in *Easy Does It*.

MOVEABLE CHORDS

6th String Root Chords major, minor, dominant 7th

The *Challenge* section of this book has presented full bar, moveable **6th string root** major and dominant 7th chords (see pages 85 and 93). These chords are reviewed here and the minor chord form is added. The root (R) of these chords is located on the 6th string which will help you to identify the chords.

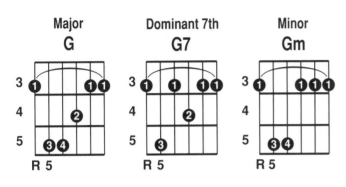

Major
G

Dominant 7th
G7

Minor
Gm

When playing all **full bar** chords, there should be slightly more pressure than normal on the side of the index finger (away from the fret and toward the nut of the guitar). Place the thumb opposite the index finger.

The following chart will help you locate and identify **MOVEABLE ROOT 6th STRING CHORDS**.

NOTE NAME 6th String ⑥	E	F	F♯/G♭	G	G♯/A♭	A	A♯/B♭	B	C
FRET	open	1	2	3	4	5	6	7	8

5th String Root Chords major, minor, dominant 7th

A moveable **5th string root** dominant 7th chord was presented in the *Challenge* on pages 73 and 93. Major and minor 5th string root chord forms are added here. The root (R) of these chords is located on the 5th string, which will help you to identify the chords.

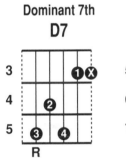

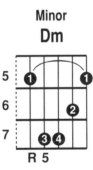

Dominant 7th
D7

Minor
Dm

To play the moveable D minor chord, bar the 5th fret with your index finger. You do not need to cover the 6th string. The pressure on the index finger should be on the side of the finger nearest the nut of the guitar.

The moveable **D chord** requires a *3rd finger bar* technique. Place the 3rd finger on the 4th, 3rd, 2nd and 1st strings. Damp (❌) the 1st string by arching the finger. Now place the index finger on the 5th string. The pressure on the 3rd finger needs to be on the side on the finger toward the fret (just the opposite of the full bar technique). To assist in helping you roll the 3rd finger toward the fret, place the thumb below (toward the nut) rather than opposite the index finger.

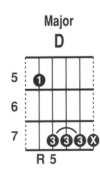

Major
D

The following chart will help you locate and identify moveable **ROOT 5TH STRING CHORDS**.

NOTE NAME 5th String ⑤	A	A♯/B♭	B	C	C♯/D♭	D	D♯/E♭	E	F
FRET	open	1	2	3	4	5	6	7	8

Principal Chords moveable

When used together, moveable root 6th string and moveable root 5th string chords enable you to play the **PRINCIPAL CHORDS** (I, IV, V) in any key. Practice the **Principal Chords** in the keys of G, C, A minor and E minor.

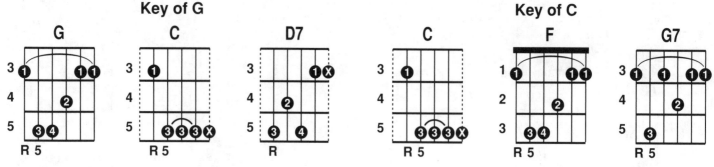

Play *Rocking the Scale* (page 62) and *Blues in G* (page 72) for practice in using moveable chords.

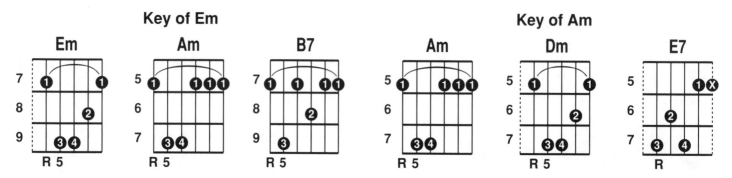

Play *Scarborough Fair* (page 55) using moveable chords in the key of A minor.

Progress to Five (page 66), *Sunday* (page 69), *New Horizons* (page 70) and *Fresh Air* (page 86) will give you some practice in playing moveable principal and secondary chords.

CHALLENGE Moveable Major and Minor 7th Chords

6th String Root Chords

Major 7th	Minor 7th
Gmaj7	Am7

5th String Root Chords

Major 7th	Minor 7th
Cmaj7	Dm7

In the **Gmaj7 chord**, dampen the 5th and 1st strings by lightly touching them with the index finger. To play the **Am7 chord**, bar the 5th fret with the index finger. Place the 3rd finger on the 5th string, 7th fret.

When playing the moveable **Cmaj7 chord**, dampen the 1st string by lightly touching it with the index finger. In the **Dm7 chord**, bar the 5th fret and then add the 2nd and 3rd fingers.

For practice in using the moveable major and minor 7th chords, play *Jazz Blues* (page 79).